NUTS AND SEEDS
THE NATURAL SNACKS

NUTS AND SEEDS
THE NATURAL SNACKS

by the Rodale Press Editors
Compiled and Prepared by Joanne Moyer

Book Division,
Rodale Press, Inc.
Emmaus, Pa. 18049

Book and Jacket design by Donald E. Breter

Standard Book Number 0-87857-064-0
Library of Congress Card Number 72-93742

Printed in the United States of America
Printed on Recycled Paper
FIRST PRINTING—July, 1973
JB-8

Contents

Introduction

Snacking used to be nutritious, appetizing and fun. People would gather around the kitchen table with a nutcracker and bowlful of almonds and walnuts or some sunflower seeds, maybe a few apple slices and a glass of cider, and enjoy. Nowadays snacking means mechanically dipping into boxes or bags of additive-ridden chips, crackers or curls that are as costly as they are unhealthful.

"Nuts and Seeds, the Natural Snacks" shows the way back to the kind of nutritious nibbling that provides plenty of vitamins, minerals and protein in every bite, with good flavor and crunchy texture to boot. It shows how readers can grow their own nuts and seeds and gives recipes for many novel ways to use them in the kitchen.

Part 1

J. I. Rodale

Seeds, as Human Food

Chapter 1

The Hidden Vitality in Seeds

J. I. Rodale was convinced that seeds and nuts (which are really seeds in a shell) are nature's own "core of life." He saw them as a delicious and prolific source of the vitamins and minerals we need to stay in good health. Since these nutrients are so lacking in the diets of most Americans, Mr. Rodale was anxious to promote an appreciation of seeds as nuggets of nutrition in the guise of interesting, tasty snacks. It is fitting that we begin our book with some of his thoughts on seeds.

The Editors

"And God said, 'Behold, I have given you every herb bearing seed, which is upon the face of the earth, and every tree, in which is the fruit of a tree yielding seed; to you it shall be for meat.' "

This is Genesis, Chapter 1, verse 29 . . . The seed is life itself. It contains the spark which is extremely vital to the functioning of our bodies. The perpetuation of the species is accomplished through the seed. The seed is the vehicle for storing life's reserves. The seed is the crucible wherein the alchemy of life works its magic. In this tiny place is contained the condensed germinating energy, the life-giving elements, including as yet undiscovered gleams. Science still knows very little of the vast and intricate interplay of life forces that lie within the seed.

Its living substance can be preserved for many years, and during the entire life of the seed, which in the case of certain legumes is more than 50 years, there is a continuous respiratory action, showing that it is a living organism. The seed of the Indian lotus plant buried for over 200 years in peat bogs has been known to germinate successfully. Melon seeds carefully stored, packed between paper, have germinated after 30 years. There must be very important life-giving elements that will resist the passage of such long periods of time and they make seeds a very healthful food for us. All seeds are rich in vitamin B, and other nutrients important in fertility. That is why wheat germ is often fed to women who do not seem to be able to bear children.

Everyone knows that vegetables are essential to a properly balanced diet, but their maximum vitamin content is only found in really fresh produce. Compare crisp lettuce straight from the garden with the limp faded thing it becomes two days later. Its "living" quality has gone, and with it, much of its food value. This cannot be said of seeds.

Proof of the Food Value of Seeds

To get an idea of what nutrition is packed in the average seed, bear in mind that nature has placed an extra store of concentrated food in it to nourish the emerging plant for a few days. There is enough food in the seed to be used by the young plant to form a root, stem and several leaves without having to get food from the soil.

Seed foods are wonderful for city folk who are faced with the necessity of eating so much processed food. They can protect themselves by making seed foods a liberal part of their diets. Seeds are also a protection in winter when one is eating stored vegetables that have lost much of their potency.

Much data is available to prove that seeds are a food of high nutritional value. In the magazine, *Science,* 1932, vol. 75, p. 294, Davidson and Chandbliss wrote an article called *Chemical Composition of Rice and Its Relation to Soil Fertility in China and Japan.* It is an astounding article of far-reaching significance to nutritionists. Davidson and Chandbliss, in experimental work, discovered that "variations in the nutrient content of soils have less effect on the seed than on any other part of the plant." The best food elements in the soil will be saved for the seed so that the plant will be sure to reproduce itself. Nature wants to be sure of that. This would indicate that seeds have a higher nutritional value than the leafy parts of the plant.

The seed must have sufficient potency to carry on into the next generation. Therefore, where there is a given amount of organic minerals available, as much of it as can possibly be spared will go to the seed. Even in an infertile soil, whatever organic minerals the roots of a plant can forage out will be available first for the formation of seed.

Professor William A. Albrecht of the University of Missouri's Department of Soils calls a seed "the means of survival of the species, hence this survival will not be possible unless a minimum of food materials are stored in the seed. We well know that when the fertility of the soil drops to a low level less seed is produced. Seemingly the amount of seed is the variable, while the quality of the seed is more nearly constant. It is the fertility of the soil as a growth-providing substance that seems to determine the seed production rather than the air, water and sunshine that contribute the starches and the energy materials."

This is an important point. If you are worried about having to purchase food raised with chemical fertilizers, see to it that a certain portion of your diet consists of seeds. The seed is not anywhere nearly as much affected by the use of strong chemicals as the leaves or stalks, and thus contains significant amounts of organic elements.

Seeds and Mental Power

Is there such a thing as brain food? It used to be that fish was thought of in that way. Nutritionists referred to the phosphorus in fish as the brain-stimulating factor. Over the years this idea has lost favor. But if there was ever any substance to the theory, then seeds are truly a brain food. They contain 10 or 20 times more phosphorus than fish does.

Animals that are fed raw grain seeds can perform much more work than those grazing exclusively on pasture grass. Of course, this is work, not brain power, but look a little further.

In *A System of Diet and Dietetics,* G. A. Sutherland, M.D., wrote: "Thus among the rodents, the rabbit, unable to climb and with little prehensile power, has to be content with a bulky diet of comparatively non-nutritious herbs, while the more intelligent squirrel, a nimble climber and possessed of considerable prehensile power, is able to procure highly nutritious seeds and a considerable amount of animal food as well. . ."

Later on, this author states, "The frugivora, which include animals like the squirrel, the rat, and the monkey, consume vegetable food in its more concentrated forms, such as seeds and nuts. Being generally more intelligent than the herbivora, they are able to pick and choose their food more cleverly; and securing it in more concentrated forms, they are provided with a much less bulky digestive system than the herbivora."

Include Seeds in Your Diet

Luther Burbank, the great plant wizard, realized the value of the seed as human food. In his book, *Partner of Nature* (Appleton-Century, 1939), he stated, "Fruits ripen, not to make food for us, but to encase and protect the seeds inside—pips or pits or kernels. But we pay no attention to Nature's purpose and revel in the delicate flavors and delicious flesh of apples, pears, peaches, tomatoes, melons and all and throw aside carelessly the seeds that the plant went to so much trouble to build and in which it stored the life-giving germ and a reserve of starch to help it start in life again as a baby plant."

Dr. Henry C. Sherman, Columbia University's outstanding nutritional authority, has said that in studying the nutritional needs of man you cannot deal exclusively in terms of known chemical factors. You have to include "natural articles of food" he says, "to ensure adequate supplies of any possible factors which may not yet have been identified and listed in chemical terms. We must give emphasis to those foods which, as the 'natural wholes' to which our species is nutritionally adjusted by its evolutionary history, will furnish us, along with the known essentials, any unknown factors which may also be essential to our nutrition." Could Dr. Sherman have been referring to seeds? They certainly are "natural wholes."

Chapter 2

Seeds, down through the Centuries

In the primitive days of civilization, a goodly part of man's diet was in the form of seeds consumed without any cooking, tampering or processing. In Biblical times a great deal of seed food was part of the daily diet. Dill and cumin seeds were considered so important that tithes were paid with them.

In his book, *Jewish Magic and Superstition,* Rabbi Trachtenberg says that Baladur (Anacardia, the family of trees and shrubs that includes the cashew, mango, pistachio and sumac) is a memory-strengthener. He advises for further strengthening of the memory, "Eat hazelnuts for nine days, beginning with six and adding six more each day; eat pepper seeds for nine days, beginning with one seed and doubling the dose until it reaches 256 seeds on the ninth day, and each time before you consume them, recite Deuteronomy 33:8-11 and Psalm 119:9-16; grind cloves, long peppers, dates, ginger, ga-langa-root, and muscot nuts in equal quantities, beat them with olive oil into a paste, and eat a little every morning before breakfast."

The Romans, at the end of their gluttonous feasts, ate spice cakes flavored with aniseed. Cakes charged with a large variety of seeds were a standby of the Middle Ages. Vernon Quinn, in *Seeds—Their Place in Life and Legend,* describes an Englishman of Pepys' time who commended seeds as "marvel-ously good for a melancholicke person, excellent fine for such as be of a cholericke nature even to free the sleep from monstrous nocturnal visions."

There seems to be some evidence of a depend-ence on eating seed in those days, either to strengthen the mind (free it from conditions brought about by dissipation), or to cheer it up generally. Common sense tells us that the mind is nourished by the food we eat, and that seed food, which contains so much potent, living quality, must be an excellent means of maintaining its health.

The American Indians, Seed Eaters

Aside from meat, seeds were perhaps the main-stay of diet among the American Indians. Many of the seed foods with which we are so familiar today originated with the Indians. Corn, or maize, is one of these.

Wrote Sir Walter Raleigh of the new land, America, "I tell thee, 'tis a goodlie country, not wanting in victuals. On the banks of those rivers are divers fruits good to eat and game aplenty. Besides, the natives in those parts have a corne, which yields them bread; and this with little labor and in abundance. 'Tis called in the Spanish tongue 'mahiz.' "

As important a food as corn naturally figured largely in the folklore of the Indians. Placing corn or other grain on the grave to feed the soul of the deceased was a common Indian custom. The Naragansetts believed that long ago a crow came to their ancestors bearing a bean and a kernel of corn, an event which marked the beginning of their farming. As a result they would never drive a crow away from their cornfields. Was he not the father of their agriculture?

The Indians had figured out just about every possible way to eat corn: They ate it roasted, right from the stalk, as we sometimes do today; they picked it green, pressed out some of the milk from the kernels, and boiled the corn in this milk; they dried the mature ears and ground the kernels into meal which was the staple food for winter. On long journeys Indians carried no provisions with them, except a bag of parched, ground corn which, along with whatever meat they could find in the forests, sustained them during the entire journey.

The Plains Indians added cornsilk to their cornmeal. They thought it added sweetness to the taste. Many Indians sucked the juicy stalks of the corn as they gathered the ears. The Hurons had a unique way of preparing the cereal. They soaked young corn

Cornsilk added a sweetness to the taste of cornmeal as prepared by the Indians.

ears in water until they were putrid, then boiled this evil-smelling soup and drank it. Knowing what we know today about yeasts and molds, this was probably a very healthful procedure, after all. Other Indians burned the corncob to ashes and mixed the ashes with their corn dishes—an excellent way to preserve all the minerals.

Samp was Indian mush, which was eaten either hot or cold. Succotash, corn and beans together, was a favorite dish.

Sunflower Seeds

Sunflower seeds were, and still are, a favorite Indian food. "There is a greate herbe in the forme of a Marigold," wrote an early author, "some take it to bee *Planta Solis:* of the seeds therefore they make both a kinde of bread and broth." Since the sun was worshipped extensively in Indian religions, it is understandable that the sunflower should be held in great esteem: it follows the sun, turning its head across the sky through all the hours of the day.

The sunflower is still cultivated by the Hopi Indians today. The seeds were more than just a source of food to the early Hopis. The color was extracted from the great purple seeds, peculiar to the Hopi sunflowers, to make a dye. In addition to the cultivated sunflower, the Hopis also used the many wild sunflowers that grew near their villages. The flowers of the wild sunflower plant were supposed to be a medicine for spider bites.

The Importance of Acorns

Acorns, the seed of the oak tree, were a major food for many Indian nations. Says Mark Graubard in his book, *Man's Food,* "Our earliest known bread was made from acorns and beechnuts. Some American Indians on the Pacific coast prepared cakes from crushed acorns even in post-Columbian days. This fruit contains a bitter substance which primitive man learned quickly enough to extract and dissolve. Indians washed the acorn meal in boiling water for several hours, to eliminate the bitter-tasting substance. The remaining meal was dried in the sun and baked in its warmth or over a hot fire."

Indians used to extract oil from acorns and use it either as a hairdressing or in food. Acorns were gathered regularly by squaws and old men among the Californians (Indians), and the invariable sound that salutes the ear as one approaches a village is the monotonous thump-thump of the pestles used by the women in pounding the acorn into flour. The Californians dedicated a special ceremonial dance to the acorn.

Other Nuts

Nuts of all kinds were important to the Indians. According to an early authority, Indians used to shell black walnuts by breaking them between two stones; then they dried the kernels in the sun and ground them in a mortar. Water was poured over the finely crushed walnuts and the tiny pieces of shell would sink to the bottom. The water, taking up flavor and

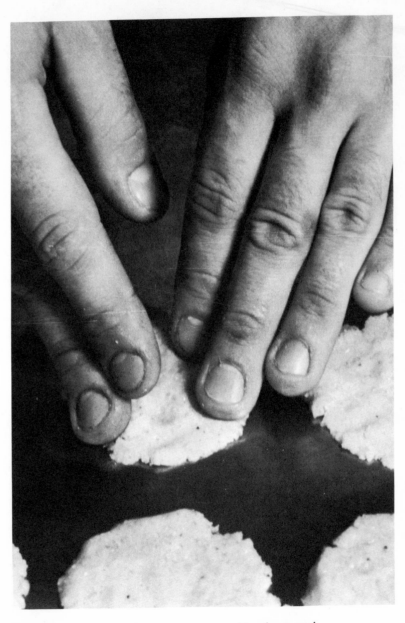

Pacific Coast Indians made a coarse acorn-and-beechnut meal which may have been the base of the earliest known bread.

substances from the nuts, became walnut milk—a tasty addition to a variety of dishes.

We are also indebted to the Indians of North, Central or South America for the following seed-foods: squash, peanuts, Brazil nuts, pecans, vanilla, wild rice, kidney and lima beans, mesquite beans, pinon nuts, cashews, watermelon, cactus and all of the cereals. The Indians also made use of the following seeds, which we do not generally use: amarinth, brickeye, chia, goosefoot, islay, jojoba, juniper, chick-apins, salt-bush, song-wae, tarweed, wild flax, wild sage.

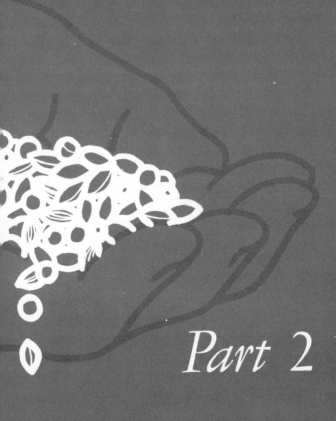

Part 2

Nutrition and
Prevention of Disease

Chapter 3

Seeds Are a Sensational Food

Stop to think about it, and you will see that a seed is the very core of life. Within its tiny kernel it contains a mysterious, concentrated storehouse of energy and nutrients designed by nature, the master chemist, to nourish a seedling plant.

How do seeds really stack up against other foods from a nutritive point of view? They comprise a very necessary and important part of a healthy diet.

Phosphorus in Seeds

Phosphorus is the mineral which abounds in seeds. You have to eat a bushel of apples or half a bushel of oranges to get the amount of phosphorus contained in one pound of lentils or beans, wheat or oats. These last are all, of course, seeds.

Phosphorus is important to body functions and is present in all body cells. Calcium and phosphorus stand first and second respectively in the quantity of mineral elements in the body. The body's use of phosphorus is closely related to its use of calcium; the amount of phosphorus needed by the body depends on the amount of calcium present. The proper ratio is two-and-a-half to one—there should be two-and-a-half times as much calcium as phosphorus.

People who live chiefly on fruits and vegetables are likely to suffer from a lack of phosphorus or from an incorrect calcium to phosphorus ratio unless they include meat, cereals or nuts in their diet.

Phosphorus is present in bones and teeth, along with calcium, and is an important component of brain tissue. Phosphorus also appears in the body's fluids and soft tissues. It combines with protein, to aid in protein digestion. In addition, the body needs phosphorus to process several of the important B vitamins.

Other Minerals in Seeds

All seeds are naturally rich in iron. The iron is removed from cereal grains with the germ in the refining process. So the processing of wheat and other grains becomes a significant factor in the statistics which show that most American women and many adolescents suffer from some form of iron-deficiency anemia.

The diets of many Americans are deficient in magnesium, another of the minerals lost in food processing. In listings of magnesium-rich foods, the highest are mostly all seed foods. For example, those that rate high (from 120 to 250 milligrams per hundred grams) are: almonds, barley, lima beans, Brazil nuts, cashew nuts, corn, whole wheat flour, hazelnuts, oatmeal, peanuts, peas, pecans, brown rice, soy flour, walnuts. Apparently magnesium is essential to a seed as it grows into a mature plant, or why would nature have packed so much of this mineral into each kernel?

Magnesium is absolutely essential to humans for the formation of strong bones and teeth and healthy nerves and blood vessels. It even has a beneficial effect on the blood cholesterol level, according to Professor Ancel Keys, noted research scientist and director of the University of Minnesota's Laboratory of Physical Hygiene. In animals on controlled diets a magnesium deficiency leads to dilated blood vessels, kidney damage, hair loss, rough, sticky coats, diarrhea and edema.

This is the vital mineral that is removed from grains when they are refined.

Zinc is one of the trace minerals in seeds that triggers the action of many enzymes and vitamins. Dr. Walter Pories, a pioneer in zinc research, calls zinc "the mineral for men" because it is so vital to the development of the male sex glands. Zinc also promotes healing and heart and prostate health.

Vitamins in Seeds

Among the most precious food elements in nuts, legumes and seeds are the B vitamins and vitamin E. Apparently young plants need these vitamins just as we do. Some seeds contain more of the vitamin B complex than a like amount of wheat germ (usually considered one of the best sources of B vitamins). One hundred grams of sunflower seeds contain as much as 5.8 milligrams of niacin, 1.96 milligrams of thiamine, and .23 milligrams of riboflavin. The B vitamins are important for healthy nerves, healthy skin, and efficient functioning of the digestive system.

Vitamin E is absolutely essential for heart health and for smooth functioning of all reproductive processes, especially for preventing sterility, miscarriage, and difficult births. It is also of value in preventing internal blood clots. Up to 31 International Units (I.U.) of alpha tocopherol and 222 milligrams of mixed tocopherols are present in every three-and-a-half ounces of seeds.

For a beautiful complexion, for good eyesight, and for healthy mucous membranes we need vitamin A, another nutrient plentiful in seeds. Every 100 grams of sunflower seed kernels contains about 50 I.U. of vitamin A.

A Rich Source of Vitamin F

The natural oils in seeds are remarkable sources of the essential fatty acids, vitamin F. We all need vitamin F if we are to have smooth, beautiful skin and healthy hair. We need it to improve our resistance to disease because it helps to build strong connective tissue in the cells. Vitamin F is especially important in maintaining a healthy reproductive system. According to English nutritionist Dr. Hugh Sinclair, this vitamin helps to prevent bronchial asthma, rheumatoid arthritis and ulcers. A wide variety of disorders—eczema, dry skin, dandruff, brittle nails, hair loss, kidney disease, and prostate gland diseases —may be caused by a lack of these important fats in the diet.

Fats are carried by a substance called lecithin, abundant in the fatty portions of seeds. Lecithin dissolves easily in body fluids, so that the fats can be properly distributed. Cholesterol, the fatty substance present in different kinds of foods and manufactured in the body as well, is kept in a state of emulsion by lecithin so that the body can use it. Without lecithin, cholesterol is likely to collect in the walls of blood vessels and interfere with circulation.

When you have no seeds in your diet, or if you eat only seed foods from which the lecithin has been removed by processing, you sacrifice a valuable weapon against developing a cholesterol problem.

Seed Snacks for Protein

Protein is the chief substance of which we are made. Blood, organs, skin, hair, nails, bones and body fluids are all protein. Our brain and our nerves are protein. Protein is made up of individual kinds of "building blocks"—the amino acids. There are often more than 20 various kinds of acids present in certain foods we eat. Our digestive processes rearrange the amino acids, building them into body structures—brain, nerves or skin, for example.

Certain of the amino acids are absolutely necessary. We must have them to survive. These so-called essential amino acids have names like arginine, lysine, methionine, tryptophan and valine. We cannot manufacture the essential amino acids—they must be supplied by the foods we eat. One reason seeds are so valuable as a snack food is that their high content of the essential amino acids occurs in *balanced* amounts not usually found in any food but meat and fish.

Most of us get far, far too little protein. The adult man should have about 70 grams of protein every day. The average woman, 60. The requirement for children ranges from 40 (for one to three-year-olds) to 100 grams a day for boys from 16 to 20. Protein food is generally the most expensive food. In addition, it is often crowded out of our diets by refined carbohydrates—candy, cake and soda.

Add protein to your diet using the seed foods; seed protein is fairly inexpensive. Don't rely on seeds in place of good meat and egg protein, but do use them as a substitute for "worthless" snack foods. Even though seeds are not "complete" protein, in the sense of having *all* the essential amino acids, they can add a great deal to the total protein you get in any one day.

Look at the following chart showing the mineral and vitamin content of the most common seed foods. Nutritionally speaking, do you think you can afford to do without a good supply of these foods in their fresh, unrefined, untampered-with state?

THE NUTRITIVE CONTENT OF SOME SEED FOODS

Seed	Cal-ories	Pro-tein Grams	Fat Grams	Total Car-bohyd. Grams	Cal-cium Mgs.	Phos-phorous Mgs.	Iron Mgs.	Sodium Mgs.	Potas-sium Mgs.	A I.U.	Thia-min Mgs.	Ribo-flavin Mgs.	Niacin Mgs.	C Mgs.	E Mgs.	K Mgs.	Average Portions Measure
Grains:																	
Barley, pearled	711	17	2	161	33	386	4.1	6.12	326	0	2.4	1.6	6.3	0	6.5-10.8		1 cup
Buckwheat Flour	341	6.3	1.1	77.9	10.8	86	.98			0	.08	.04	.4	0			1 cup
Cornmeal, whole	459	18.4	4.3	94.5	7.6	226	2.3			558	.4	.10	2.4	0	3-12		1 cup
Millet	332	6.2	1.4	78.2	329	254	5.3	.7	131		.33	.10	1.3				1 cup
Oatmeal, cooked	150	5.5	2.9	26.1	21.4	160	1.7				2.4	.05	.5	0	4.8		1 cup
Rice, brown	748	15.6	3.5	161.6	81	630	4.2	18.7	312	0	.67	.10	9.7	0	4.9		1 cup
Rice, converted	677	14.2	.6	148	44.8	254	1.5	7.5	318	0	.37	.07	7.1	0	.74		1 cup
Rice, wild	593	23	1.1	123	30.9	552		11.4	358	0	.73	1.03	10.1	0	.76		1 cup
Rye flour, dark	254	13	2	54.5	43.2	429	3.6	.8	108	0	.49	.18	2.2	0	1.8-2.8		1 cup
Sesame seed	610	19.3	51.1	18.1	1,125	614	9.5				.93	.22	4.5	0			100 grams
Sorghum	332	11.0	3.3	73.0	28	287	4.4				.38	.15	3.9		2.2-3.5	2.4	1 cup
Wheat flour	400	11.5	1.1	83.7	17.6	9.6	3.2	1.1	95	0	.48	2.9	3.9	0		2.4	1 cup
Wheat germ	246	17	6.8	33.7	57.1	745	5.5	1.4	530	0	1.39	.54	3.12	0		2.5	1 cup
Vegetables:																	
Chickpeas, dry	359	20.8	4.7	60.9	162	344	8.4	.3-.4	240-370	90	.49	.18	1.6	Trace		.01	1 cup
Corn, sweet, raw	92	3.7	1.2	20.5	9	120	.5			390	.15	.12	1.7	12			1 ear
Corn, sweet, cooked	119	3.8	.98	28.2	7	73	.84			546	.15	.14	1.9	11.2			1 ear
Cowpeas	44	3.4	.3	9.2	53	65	1.1	2	560	1,520	.16	.10	1.1	34			1 cup
Lentils, dry, split	204	14.4	.72	36.2	20	175	4.4	1.8	720	342	.34	.14	1.3	3			1/4 cup
Lima beans, raw	96	5.6	.6	17.6	47	118	1.7	.75	510	210	.16	.08	1.05	24			1/2 cup
Lima beans, cooked	76	4	.32	14.6	23	62	1.4			232	.11	.07	.88	12			1/2 cup
Mung beans, sprouts	23	2.9	.2	4.1	29	59	.8			10	.07	.09	.5	15			1 cup
Mung beans, dry	339	24.4	1.4	59.7	91	320	6.3		278	40	.68	.21	2.0	3			1 cup
Peas, green, raw	74	5	.3	13.3	16.5	92	1.4	.75		510	.26	.12	2	20			1/2 cup
Peas, green, cooked	42	2.9	.24	7.3	13.2	73	1.1			432	.15	.84	1.3	9	1.6	.52	1 cup
Peas, dry, split	344	24.5	1.0	61.7	33	268	5.1	42	880	370	.77	.28	3.1	2	3.6	Fair	1/2 cup
Popcorn	54	1.8	.7	3.1	1.5	39	.38	3	33.6	70	.057	.017	.31	0			1 cup, popped
Pumpkin seed	541	30.9	43.1	17.9	33	1,290	12.7			80	.25	.13	2.0				1 cup
Red Kidney Beans, cooked	230	14.5	1	42	122	316	4.8			0	1.3	.13	2	0	3.1		1 cup
Soybean, dry	695	73	38	73	477	1,230	16.8	8.4	3,990	231	2.25	.63	4.8	Trace		39	1 cup
Soybean sprouts, raw	50	6.6	1.5	5.7	51	72	1.07			192	.25	.21	.85	14			1 cup

Do Seeds Have an Anti-Cancer Value?

Among the Indians of Taos Pueblo in New Mexico, among the Hunzakuts of Pakistan, among the Maoris of New Zealand, cancer is as rare as tigers on the streets of Manhattan.

There are primitive people (so-called) who have never seen an electric can opener, a TV dinner, or popsicles, potato chips and candy bars. Neither have they ever seen leukemia, or a case of terminal malignancy.

Dr. J. R. Nimo, the government physician in charge of supervising the islanders of Torres Strait, north of New Zealand, reported that in his 13 years with them he did not see a single case of malignancy among the entire 4,000 native population. During the same period, Dr. Nimo operated on several dozen of the 300 white people for malignancies (*Nutrition and Physical Degeneration,* American Academy of Applied Nutrition, 1950). Is there a mystery factor which gives to primitive man an immunity against this disease? Is there something we can learn from his habits which might help us to stem the tide of cancer in our own civilization?

Travelers who make the arduous trip to the land of the Hunzakuts, high in the mountains of Pakistan, are greeted warmly and offered the traditional refreshment immediately—a bowl of fresh apricots. Beside the bowl a special dish is provided for the pits. The next day, the visitor is offered the kernels.

Do these kernels have important protective powers? Is there something in the seeds of fruits—

seeds which we discard with the garbage and which primitive people make a point of consuming—which helps to keep them from cancer?

Cancer and arthritis are both reportedly rare among the Taos (New Mexico) Pueblo Indians. Their traditional beverage is made from the ground kernels of cherries, peaches and apricots. Robert G. Houston enjoyed this beverage when he was in New Mexico gathering material for a book dealing with cancer prevention. When he came home Houston began to make blender shakes based on the Indian recipe. Into a glass of milk or juice, he mixed a tablespoon of honey with freshly ground apricot kernels (one-fourth ounce or two dozen) which had been roasted for 10 minutes at 300° F. Roasting the kernels is important, Houston points out, "in order to insure safety when you are using the pits in such quantities." (Roasting destroys enzymes which could give you an upset stomach if you eat too many raw fruit seeds at one time.) The drink was delicious, so Houston kept having it daily.

On the third day of drinking this concoction he noticed that two little benign skin growths on his arm, which formerly were pink, had turned brown. Next day he was shocked to notice that both were black and shrivelled. On the seventh morning the smaller, more recent growth had vanished completely and the larger one, about the size of a grain of rice, had just simply fallen off.

Houston says that two of his friends have since tried the apricot pit shakes and report similar elimination of benign skin growths in one to two weeks.

What is there in apricot pits that has this remarkable effect? Certain foods, especially the kernels of certain fruits and grains, contain elements known as the nitrilosides (amygdalin, vitamin B_{17}), says Dr. Ernst T. Krebs, Jr., well-known biochemist and codiscoverer of Laetrile, a controversial cancer treatment. (Laetrile is the proprietary term for one nitriloside.) Nitrilosides, Dr. Krebs told the recent New England States Natural Foods Associates Convention in Manchester, Vermont, are non-toxic, water soluble, accessory food factors found in abundance in the seeds of almost all fruits. They're also found in over 1,000 other plants. Wherever primitive peoples have been found to have exceptional health, with a marked absence of malignant and degenerative disease, their diet has been shown to be high in the naturally occurring nitrilosides.

These nitrilosides, these anti-cancer vitamins, just might be to cancer what vitamin C is to scurvy, what niacin is to pellagra, what vitamin B_{12} and folic acid are to pernicious anemia, says Dr. Krebs. As he points out, "it is much, much more important to avoid the development of cancer than to have to deal with it after it has become clinically evident." The nitrilosides may well represent the key by which man can avoid the development of cancer, just as we have discovered in vitamin C the means by which man may avoid the development of scurvy or, having developed scurvy, the means to cure it in its early stages.

Since apricot kernels contain as much as 2 percent amygdalin, Houston's apricot seed cocktail provided him with one-quarter gram of nitriloside per glass, an amount which equals the basic daily B_{17} ration of cancer-free primitive people, and is one-third the daily oral dose of 700 to 800 milligrams used to control cancer by Dr. Hans Nieper of Hanover, Germany (*Alameda Times Star,* 14 July 1970).

There are other common foods (all seeds) which will provide a goodly supply of this protective factor—millet and buckwheat are two. Lentil, mung beans and alfalfa, when sprouted, provide 50 times more nitriloside than the mature plant does. Since other essential protective elements are increased in the sprouting of such seeds, young sprouts make excellent snack food ingredients. Perhaps we would do well to heed the advice of Dr. Earnest A. Hooton of Harvard University who said in *Apes, Men, and Morons,* "Let us to the ignorant savage, consider his way of eating and be wise."

Sunflower seeds—a delicious, concentrated bit of nourishment.

Chapter 4

Sunflower Seeds: The Super Snack

J. I. Rodale

In the latter part of 1941, Deaf Smith County, Texas, gained national fame as the county whose inhabitants had teeth superior to any known anywhere in the world. The people in and around Hereford displayed teeth so remarkably healthy that the incidence of dental caries was almost completely nil. It was found that the soil in the Hereford area was rich in lime and phosphorus and contained some fluorine. These three elements are basic to the formation of teeth and bones and, because the residents absorbed these elements through the food grown in this soil, they developed this extraordinary incidence of healthy teeth and bones.

Dr. S. G. Harootian of the Worcester State Hospital in Massachusetts, after hearing about Deaf

Smith County, immediately began investigations into the possibility of finding a food containing all three elements. After much research and experimentation, he found that the bones of beef cattle ground fine as flour would serve the intended purpose. In an astounding nine-month experiment with nine mental patients, the formation of cavities was absolutely arrested by the addition of bone meal to their diets.

I Check on the Food Value of Sunflower Seeds

As a spectator I was irresistibly fascinated by these momentous happenings. For several years we had been growing sunflowers on our farm and feeding the seeds of this plant to our chickens. Poultry authorities speak highly of this seed as a conditioner for barnyard fowl. Parrots live almost exclusively on sunflower seeds and seem to lead a contented existence. We had never thought of eating these seeds ourselves, but when I heard about Deaf Smith County and Dr. Harootian's ingenious experiment, the thought occurred to me to check on the food-value analysis of sunflower seeds. To my amazement the ash of the seed showed a tremendous quantity of phosphorus (35 percent), calcium ($7\frac{1}{2}$ percent) and a trace of fluorine.

My Health Improves

I started to eat the seeds, a couple of heaping handfuls every day, but did not change anything else in my diet. My dentist had found only one tiny tooth cavity in about three years, so I wasn't thinking in terms of dental improvement.

About a week later a slight intermittent quiver in my left eye went away. I usually suffered from this only in the winter when there was little opportunity for exercise or sunshine. I am glad to report that it has not returned, thanks to the fact that I still eat sunflower seeds practically every day.

My eyes are not my strongest point. In the winter I would have trouble walking on snow-blanketed roads as the excessive brightness of the snow interfered with my vision. In fact, it made the snow seem a pink color.

After being on the sunflower diet for about a month, I noticed I could walk in the snow without distress. Sometime later my car broke down and I had to walk over a mile on a snowed-up highway in bright sunshine. I had no trouble at all for the first three-quarters of the way; on the last stretch my eyes smarted a little.

I noticed also that my skin seemed to be getting smoother. This doesn't seem too unreasonable because calcium and the right kind of oils are specifics for a good, strong epidermis, and the oil found in sunflower seeds is especially rich.

There are many reasons why the sunflower seed is a valuable food and should be included in everyone's daily diet. In the first place nature protects it with a casing. It, therefore, stores well and loses very little vitamin value for long periods. When you remove the outer shell you have a concentrated bit of healthy nourishment. It tastes almost as delicious a year after harvesting as on the day it was cut down. I have eaten with relish raw wheat seed on harvest

The hearty sunflower follows the sun as it travels across the sky.

day, but a month later it has already lost some of its palatability.

Secondly, you eat the sunflower seed raw. Nutritionists all agree that cooking, however skillfully done, destroys some vitamins.

This plant is one of the easiest to grow. You never hear of anyone spraying poisons on it: it is very hardy and is highly resistant to disease.

Now we come to a very remarkable fact about the sunflower. As soon as the head is formed it always faces the sun. This is a phenomenon called *heliotropism*. In the morning the head faces the east. As the sun swings in its orbit across the heavens, the sunflower head turns with it gradually, until, late in the afternoon, it is facing due west to absorb the few last rays of the dying sun. Sometime before the sun comes up next morning the head turns completely back to start the process all over again. In other words it is just drenched with sun-vitality. Perhaps that is the reason the sunflower wards off the diseases which plague other plants. Another possible reason for the potency of this little seed is that from such a small speck, there comes in a few weeks' time quite a quantity of green material, much greater than that of other food crop plants in proportion to size of seed. Nature, therefore, must pack this tiny kernel full of powerful stuff.

In the United States it is sometimes grown as a border to beautify a garden and the seeds are later thrown away. A friend of mine admitted to this crime. He didn't know whether you eat the seed shelled or with its jackets. I have since discovered many other persons who were guilty of the same uncertainty. You throw away the shell, of course.

The American Indian found copious use for the seed of the sunflower. Members of the Lewis and Clark Expedition found much evidence of this. In their journal for July 17, 1805, when they were in Montana, there is recorded the following:

"Along the bottoms, which have a covering of high grass, we observe the *sunflower* blooming in great abundance. The Indians of the Missouri, more especially those who do not cultivate maize, make great use of the seed of this plant for bread, or in thickening their soup. They first parch and then pound it between two stones, until it is reduced to a fine meal. Sometimes they add a portion of water, and drink it thus diluted; at other times they add a sufficient proportion of marrow-grease to reduce it to the consistency of common dough, and eat it in that manner. This last composition we preferred to all the rest, and thought it at that time a very palatable dish."

Note the use of marrow-grease, a product made from bones. Columbus noted how popular the sunflower was with the Indians and was instrumental in introducing it into Europe. Today, while this seed is so popular in many parts of Europe, it is practically unknown in this country as a food for humans.

Sunflower Seeds Are a Super Snack

The striking sunflower plant brings us, as gardeners, delight and beauty throughout the summer. But more important, in autumn we can harvest the seeds of this beautiful flower and, along with them, the growth-driving energy which Nature crammed into the sunflower seed.

To a large extent this is true of all seeds of life, whether fertile eggs from a chicken, the whole grain of wheat, or the simple peanut. But sunflower seeds are exceptional. It would be hard to name a single food from any source that can compare with the sunflower for providing us with such a wide range and generous amounts of nutrients. Protein, vitamins, minerals, fats, fiber, and calories—they're all there ready to go to work for you in a delicious seed. However, one of the most valuable attributes of the sunflower seed is that it's especially rich in just those nutrients in which many people tend to be deficient.

Another way to look at sunflower seeds is that they offer special rewards to people at every season of life—children, young adults, and the mature.

A Pocketful of Polly Seeds

You can eat sunflower seeds raw, just as they come from the flower. If you grow your own and husk them with your teeth, they are nothing more or less than the old-fashioned treat, "polly seeds."

You cannot talk to any Russian about sunflower seeds without having him go into ecstatic raptures on the subject. On holidays Russians will walk the streets and promenade the parks with their pockets bulging with sunflower seeds. In Russia the sunflower is a big business. There are many factories there for extracting the oil from these seeds and for making potash from the stalks. . . In the old Czar's days in Russia, every soldier in the field received what was known as iron rations. It consisted of a bag of sunflower seeds weighing one kilogram. The soldiers sometimes lived exclusively on these seeds. The army evidently was aware that they contained important nutritional values.

The only regrettable thing about sunflower seeds is that it's hard to eat a lot of them because of their diminutive size and the need to chew them up. However, by munching on them throughout the day, as Russians do, you can put away a respectable amount. On the other hand, because of their natural fiber, sunflower seeds tend not to be completely digested, so you will not actually get the full amount of nutrition that the food value charts specify. But don't feel you're being cheated, because it's worth losing some of the nutrients to gain the fiber.

To put the sunflower seed into some kind of perspective as a source of nutrients, consider that the seeds offer 920 milligrams of potassium per 100 grams (about a quarter of a pound), while bananas and oranges, usually thought of as excellent potassium sources, contain only 370 and 200 milligrams, respectively. As a source of polyunsaturated linoleic acid, sunflowers are unequaled by any other easily available whole food. Fiber? Sunflower seeds have 3.8 milligrams per 100 grams of seed. By way of comparison, meat has zero fiber, carrots one milligram and walnuts 2.1. As for protein, sunflower seeds are actually comparable to meat.

Chapter 5

Sesame Seed: Ancient and Nutritious Legacy

Sesame was among the earliest seed crops cultivated by man. Legends from the East speak as casually of sesame seed as western stories speak of peas or beans. Products made from this little but mighty seed formed a nutritional base in the diets of many ancient races. The seeds were an easy-to-carry-along snack. In addition, the tasty sesame was used as flavoring in cakes, candy and other foods.

Sesame seeds provide a factor (sometimes called vitamin T) which is important to the health of the spleen, the organ which filters and stores blood. Chances are you have never heard of vitamin T. You will not find any at the drugstore, or even at the health food store. Sometimes called Goetsch's vitamin, vitamin T is a complex of growth-promoting substances, originally obtained from termites. The termite is not exactly a favorite character, but he does have remarkable qualities of endurance and toughness.

We don't have to depend on the termite for vitamin T. This same combination of growth-promoting factors is encased in the tiny little sesame seed, the only important source of vitamin T for human use. (Very small amounts are present in organ meats, such as liver and spleen.)

For many years medical researchers considered the spleen a vestigial organ that humans can live without very nicely. Surgeons removed the spleen at the first hint of trouble. Later they discovered that the spleen plays a very important role in fighting bacterial infections, especially in children. It also helps the body to defend itself against radiation hazards, according to Professor M. W. Wintrobe, head of the Department of Medicine of the University of Utah and Director of the Laboratory of Study of Heredity and Metabolic Disorders (*International Forum,* vol. 3, no. 9).

Today doctors know that the spleen influences blood circulation and the production of certain blood cells. It is the disposal depot for worn-out red cells. A healthy spleen is certainly important and that's where the sesame seed comes in, by providing vitamin T.

Sesame and the Tough Turks

The Turks and the Greeks, once considered the toughest soldiers in war, carried sesame seed with them at all times. It was their K-ration. Turkish soldiers, it is said, showed an unusual capacity to deal with suffering under stress.

Apparently there is some mysterious quality in vitamin T which promotes and encourages appetite. When used to strengthen the lifeline of premature babies in 1953, it produced marvelous results. Dr. H. Schmidt presented his observations (*Die Medizinische Stuttgart*) on the use of vitamin T for 28 premature infants and 52 full-term infants whose development was retarded. He administered five drops of the vitamin T preparation twice daily to weak, premature babies. To older babies he gave 10 drops twice daily; later three times daily. The preparation was usually given in milk. One premature infant who weighed only 1,300 grams (2.09 pounds) received the treatment for eight weeks, but most of the other children received vitamin T for nine to 21 days.

Apparently, vitamin T fanned the breath of life in these tiny babies. Schmidt reported that they showed a tendency to increase in weight where previously their weight gain was almost nil. And while premature babies frequently show intolerance to many foods, this vitamin preparation was well tolerated. Their stools remained normal and no intestinal disturbances resulted, even in the weakest premature infants.

In another study of infants whose progress was subnormal, there were more consistent weight gains and there was a 15 percent increase in hemoglobin, the oxygen-carrying pigment of red blood corpuscles, sometimes in short supply in infants. The livid skin of the infants became normal and muscle tone was very definitely improved when the vitamin T was used, according to E. Schiff and C. Herschberger, who reported on their findings in the *Journal of the American Medical Association* (110, 3-244, 1938). These researchers also found that 20 drops a day of sesame oil administered to healthy children doubled the platelet count in three to four weeks. It seems that sesame oil could be used to good advantage in those suffering from thrombocytopenic purpura, a disease in which the blood platelets are much reduced. This is also a disease in which spleen malfunction is implicated.

The mysterious vitamin T is only one factor which makes the sesame seed so aptly deserving of the aphorism "little but mighty." High in protein, rich in polyunsaturates that are so good for the heart and blood vessels, sesame seeds, sesame oil, and tahini (sesame butter) can be the key to improved health. There are indications it might also contribute to long life.

In Turkey, for instance, where sesame seed products are a long-established part of the food pattern, many people live to see their 100th birthday. Tahini is used in Turkey as we use butter here. Turks spread it on bread, use it as a shortening for cookies and cakes, and combine it with honey to make the delicious confection Halvah.

Sesame products can, in fact, open the door to heart health and to freedom from cholesterol problems. The sesame seed is a valuable source of easily-digested, lecithin-rich fats, including the important unsaturated fatty acids which, due to food processing, are so desperately lacking in modern diets.

Sesame lecithin is considered by some to be superior even to soybean lecithin. Raymond Bernard, Ph.D., pointed out many years ago that lecithin in sesame seeds is provided in the form of an emulsion which is easier for the body to handle than non-emulsified forms of soybean lecithin (*Nature's Path,* March, 1956).

The effectiveness of sesame-derived lecithin might well be due to the fact that sesame, besides being especially rich in the two B vitamins, inositol and choline, is extremely high in methionine, one of the amino acids or building blocks of protein that is scarce in most foods of vegetable origin. Soybeans, for instance, considered a high protein vegetable, contain only half as much methionine as sesame seeds do. (*Composition of Foods Used in Far Eastern Countries,* Agriculture Handbook No. 34, U.S. Department of Agriculture.) Every cell in the body requires methionine. When there is more than enough to supply the demands of the cells, the excess is converted into choline, which is frequently deficient in American diets. A choline deficiency can seriously impede the body's ability to handle cholesterol. It can also slow down the furnace in which the body produces energy instead of fat (G. Clement *et al., Archives of Scientific Physiology,* 11, 101, 1957). Sesame products, then, are certainly a boon to heart health and to freedom from those cholesterol deposits that cause so many other problems.

Another outstanding virtue of sesame seed is its extremely high content of calcium, coupled with the fact that it contains almost twice as much calcium as phosphorus. That's very close to the ratio in which the body best utilizes these two essential minerals. Most seed foods are high in phosphorus and low in calcium.

Sesame seed contains 1,125 milligrams or about a fourth of a pound of calcium for every 100 grams of seed (*Composition of Foods . . .*). Compare this with the calcium content of other calcium-rich foods: soybeans, 227 milligrams; Swiss cheese 1,086 milligrams; a pint of milk, 590 milligrams; a quarter pound of almonds, 230 milligrams. Sesame milk is an excellent substitute for the dairy product, which causes allergic reactions in many people.

Alkaline Protein

There is yet another remarkable feature about this remarkable seed. It contains over 35 percent protein.

"It is remarkable," Dr. M. A. Brandon points out in *Nature's Path,* March, 1958, "because of the fact that while meat, eggs, . . . and other protein foods tend to be acid-forming due to the toxic end-products of protein metabolism . . . the sesame seed, because of its high content of calcium and other minerals, while supplying an abundance of protein of high biological value, does not have this (acid-forming) effect.

"In fact," adds Dr. Brandon, "when used as a meal, cream or butter, it is one of the most digestible and alkaline protein foods known to science, [and] . . . can be handled by persons whose digestive organs are not strong enough to handle other foods. . ."

Add all the qualities of sesame in various forms (milk, meal, cream, butter) to the fact that the seed itself makes such a delightful contribution to any nuts-and-seeds snack bowl, and it is indeed a wonder that we don't make more use of this remarkable seed.

Pumpkin seeds (top and bottom) blend with sunflower seeds (right and left) and pecans (center) to make an appetizing party snack.

Chapter 6

Pumpkin Seeds and Prostate Gland Disorders

A great many American men over the age of 50 have some difficulty with their prostate, the small gland in which sperm cells are stored. During and after middle age the prostate may swell, a condition called hypertrophy. Because of the gland's location this swelling causes pain during urination and eventual urine accumulation and infection in the bladder.

The usual treatment is medication, massage or an operation to remove the gland. Dr. D. W. Devrient, of Berlin has proposed that eating pumpkin seeds is a way to prevent prostate gland disorders.

According to Dr. Devrient, the weakened prostate gland enlarges in trying to make up for the slow-down in production of male sex hormones as a man grows older. Dr. Devrient does not approve of giving hormone substances to make up for this deficiency.

"One gains the impression that artificial hormones favor the evolution of cancer rather than preventing it," he says. "In view of the fact that, with the exception of operative urology . . . and physical therapy, modern medicine has not been able to find any successful weapon against the early attrition and deterioration of the prostate gland, we have no other recourse than to seek prevention in the realm of healing plants."

Dr. Devrient found he could cure patients of prostatic trouble by having them eat pumpkin seeds. Why pumpkin seeds? According to the doctor's article, which appeared in *Heilkunde Heilwege* (January, 1959), there is almost no incidence of enlarged prostate or other prostate disorders in countries where the men eat pumpkin seeds in great quantities throughout life.

He refers to the pumpkin seed as ". . . a till-now little noticed disease-preventive plant whose rejuvenating powers for men are extolled with praise by popular medicine both in America and in Europe."

Dr. Devrient believes that the seeds contain the building materials for male hormones. Thus they supply the body indirectly, although naturally, with the means of protecting and continuing the work of the male hormones.

"The plain people knew the open secret of pumpkin seeds," he adds, "a secret which was handed down from father to son for generations . . . the Hungarian gypsy, the mountain-dwelling Bulgarian, the Anatolian Turk, the Ukrainian, the Transylvanian German—all knew that pumpkin seeds promote prostate gland health. These people eat pumpkin seeds the way Russians eat sunflower seeds: as an inexhaustible source of vigor offered by Nature.

"My assertion of the . . . influence of pumpkin seeds is based on the positive judgment of old-time doctors, but also no less on my own personal observations throughout the years. This plant has scientifically determined effects on intermediary metabolism and diuresis (excessive urination), but these latter are of secondary importance in relation to its regenerative, invigorative and vitalizing influences. There is involved herein a native plant hormone, which affects our own hormone production in part by substitution, in part by direct proliferation (production of new growth). Anyone who has studied this influence among peasant peoples has been again and again astonished at the beneficial effects of this plant."

Several French doctors have prevented and cured prostate disease by using magnesium compounds. Pumpkin seeds are very rich in magnesium. One book on the subject is *Equilibre Minéral et Santé*, (*Mineral Equilibrium and Health*), by Dr. Joseph Favier (*Librairie de Francois*, Paris).

Dr. Favier gives a Dr. Stora credit for being the first to discover magnesium chloride as an effective agent in treating urinary troubles of prostatic origin. Favier made inquiries among his physician friends who, as a result of Dr. Stora's findings, were all taking magnesium chloride. He found that four out of five of them had been disturbed by difficulties in urinating, and all of them, after taking magnesium tablets, found that their problems either diminished greatly or disappeared entirely.

Another French doctor, Chevassu, treated 12 prostatic cases with magnesium tablets, ten of whom were cured. Interestingly, the general physical condition of these patients also improved. Evidently, magnesium is necessary for overall health, as well as for adequate prostate gland performance.

Dr. Pierre Delbet has also written about magnesium helping to prevent or cure prostate troubles. He discloses in his book, *The Prevention of Cancer,* "In an earlier communication, M. Bretau and I have shown that age is accompanied by a reduction in magnesium in the most active organs, and that the absorption of halogenated salts of magnesium [magnesium combined with another element, such as chlorine] permits a struggle against certain manifestations of senility."

Dr. Delbet cites dozens of cases where prostate disease was cured with a magnesium compound. "Salts of magnesium are not medicaments," he concludes. "They are necessary food."

Zinc

The mineral zinc is very important to the health of the entire reproductive system. T. A. Mawson and M. I. Fisher, two scientists of Canada's Chalk River Atomic Project, made an exhaustive study of healthy and cancerous prostate glands, both in humans and in animals, to determine the difference in their mineral content. Reporting their results in the *Canadian Journal of Medical Sciences* (vol. 30, pp. 336-9), they explained that zinc is stored in very high quantity in the healthy prostate gland and in the sperm-nourishing seminal fluid secreted by the prostate. They found that more zinc goes into the prostate gland than into any other human tissue. More important, "There was evidence of a decreased zinc content in glands containing malignant tissue."

Surprisingly enough, pumpkin seeds, in addition to their other nutrients, are especially rich in zinc.

Have you tried all of these popular nuts—cashew, walnut, almond, Brazil nut, hazelnut, and peanuts (roasted and raw)?

Chapter 7

Health Does Grow on Trees

Nuts have more highly concentrated nutrition, measure for measure, than any other food, including meats, grains, fruits and vegetables. Nutrition-packed nuts are actually large seeds—the seeds of trees. The same life-giving spark that makes other seeds such a valuable food is also present in nuts. Nuts are so rich in protein, minerals and fat that they can serve, occasionally, as a delectable substitute for meat. Nuts certainly provide a more desirable, healthful snack than the candies and crackers that glut our markets.

One pound of oily nuts supplies 40 percent of the protein needed for each day, plus 60 percent of the phosphorus, 30 percent of the calcium and iron and four times the daily requirement of fat. A pound of nuts supplies all the calories needed for the day.

What do you think of a food that has this kind of nutritive value, grows wild and free for the picking, needs little care while it is growing, is harvested by picking it up from the ground, needs little or no processing and no cooking and keeps relatively well with no refrigeration or preservatives? Doesn't this sound like the absolutely ideal food? Why have we been so slow in recognizing nuts as one of our best and most practical snack foods?

But nuts are not just a between-meals item. They are *the* protein food among vegetarians and in the dietary habits of certain cultures. Although nuts have been somewhat neglected in America, both dietetically and agriculturally, their use as food is beginning to increase rapidly, and their cultivation is receiving attention which promises to blossom into a widepread industry. We are beginning to realize that nut trees are veritable engines of food production, just waiting to be put to work.

Speaking generally, nuts are defined as hard-shelled seeds enclosing a single, edible, oily kernel. If you want to be technical about it, you will find that nuts are classified biologically as one-seeded fruits, such as beechnut, chestnut and so forth. But we have come to think of a lot of different products as nuts, including such varied edibles as cashews, peanuts, and coconuts. Most of these are high in protein and fat and low in carbohydrates. Some nuts contain as much as 60 percent fat. Some kinds of pecans even contain as much as 76 percent fat.

Because nuts are such a copious source of calories, people who are concerned about weight gain and those who are following a special diet should eat them in moderation. For most of us, however, nuts provide a delicious whole food, solidly-packed with nutritional value.

The high fat content makes nuts an excellent food for those who are trying to gain weight. Their rich protein helps to regulate blood sugar levels, so important to good health.

Unlike ordinary crops, nut trees do not depend for sustenance on the upper crusts of farm soil which are usually subjected to artificial fertilizers and doses of arsenic, DDT and other poisons. The nutritional quality of nuts is enhanced by the deep-rooting of the trees. Roots of trees like the hickory, walnut and pecan often reach down 15 feet or more into the mineral-rich subsoil for nourishment. Even though commercially grown nuts may be treated with pesticides, they do not absorb these poisons the way ordinary fruit does. Nuts are providently protected from contamination by their shells.

Vitamins and Minerals in Nuts

Most nuts contain a good supply of vitamin A and thiamine, one of the B vitamins. (The red skin of the peanut contains considerable thiamine, so don't throw it away when you eat peanuts.) Some nuts contain vitamin E. Immature English walnuts have been found to contain large amounts of vitamin C, but it lessens as the nuts ripen.

Even though their protein content is high, nuts are not complete protein. They do not contain all of the amino acids, or kinds of protein essential for human health. All of the amino acids do not occur in any one vegetable food, except for soybeans. Even so, nuts offer an important opportunity to increase protein intake.

Most nuts taste best and are best for you when eaten straight from the shell. How digestible are raw nuts? Some authorities class them as hard on the digestion; others maintain that while many kinds of vegetable protein are difficult for the body to process, those from nuts are very easy to digest, and the nut fats (the chief food elements of nuts) are far more digestible than animal fats of any sort. Chew all nuts thoroughly to help the digestive juices do their job.

The Food Value of Nuts

Here is the nutritional composition of a number of kinds of nuts. Note that while some of them are relatively high in carbohydrates, others contain hardly any. Remember, too, that although the protein of nuts is valuable, it does not contain all of the essential amino acids present in foods of animal origin.

Source: *Composition of Foods,* Agriculture Handbook #8. United States Department of Agriculture, December, 1963.

Based on 100 grams edible portion or a 3½ oz. serving.

Name	Calories	Protein in Grams	Fat in Grams	Carbohydrate in Grams	Water %
Almond (dried)	598	18.6	54.2	19.5	4.7
Beechnut	568	19.4	50.0	20.3	6.6
Brazil nut	654	14.3	66.9	10.9	4.6
Butternut	629	23.7	61.2	8.4	3.8
Cashew	561	17.2	45.7	29.3	5.2
Chestnut (fresh)	194	2.9	1.5	42.1	52.5
Coconut (fresh)	346	3.5	35.3	9.4	50.9
Filbert (hazelnut)	634	12.6	62.4	16.7	5.8
Hickory nut	673	13.2	68.7	12.8	3.3
Lychee (raw)	64	.9	.3	16.4	81.9
Macadamia nut	691	7.8	71.6	15.9	3.0
Peanut (raw, with skin)	564	26.0	47.5	18.6	5.6
Pecan	687	9.2	71.2	14.6	3.4
Pine nut (Pignolia)	552	31.1	47.4	11.6	5.6
Pistachio	594	19.3	53.7	19.0	5.3
Walnut, black	628	20.5	59.3	14.8	3.1
Walnut, English	651	14.8	64.0	15.8	3.5

Mineral Content per 100 grams (3½) edible portion.

Name	Calcium in milligrams	Phosphorus in milligrams	Iron in milligrams	Sodium in milligrams	Potassium in milligrams	Magnesium in milligrams
Almond (dried)	234	504	4.7	4	773	270
Brazil nut	186	693	3.4	1	715	225
Butternut	...	...	6.8	..	...	...
Cashew	38	373	3.8	15*	464	267
Chestnut (fresh)	27	88	1.7	6	454	41
Coconut (fresh)	13	95	1.7	23	256	46
Filbert (hazelnut)	209	337	3.4	2	704	184
Hickory nut	trace	360	2.4	..	...	160
Macadamia nut	48	161	2.0	..	264	...
Peanut (raw, with skins)	69	401	2.1	5	674	206
Pecan	73	289	2.4	trace	603	142
Pistachio	131	500	7.3	..	972	158
Walnut, black	trace	570	6.0	3	460	190
Walnut, English	99	380	3.1	2	450	131

* unsalted nuts

The B vitamins are scarce in modern American diets, due largely to the widespread consumption of processed foods. Nuts, even in the small quantities in which we eat them, are an excellent source of the major B vitamins, as this listing shows:

Vitamin B-Complex Content per 100 grams (3½ oz.) edible portion

Name	Thiamine (B_1) in milligrams	Niacin (B_3) in milligrams	Riboflavin (B_2) in milligrams
Almonds (dried)	.24	.92	3.5
Brazil nuts	.96	.12	1.6
Cashews	.43	.25	1.8
Chestnuts (fresh)	.22	.22	.6
Coconut (fresh)	.05	.02	.5
Filberts (hazelnuts)	.46	. .	.9
Macadamia nuts	.34	.11	1.3
Peanuts			
(raw, with skins)	1.14	.13	17.2
Pecans	.86	.13	.9
Walnuts, black	.22	.11	.7
Walnuts, English	.33	.13	.9

In addition, peanuts are rich in pyridoxine, pantothenic acid and biotin, three other important members of the vitamin B family.

Pecans

Along with the other good things nuts have to offer, doctors and researchers find that some of them are effective in relieving certain diseases.

Dr. John M. Ellis, who practices medicine in northeastern Texas, has discovered that those who suffer from a form of painful neuritis and arthritis of shoulders, arms and hands, may find relief in as little as six weeks by adding 12 raw pecans per day to their diet. Dr. Ellis reported in *Peanut Journal and Nut World* (March, 1969) that he believes the relief is due to vitamin B_6, a nutrient plentiful in pecans. Meat, wheat kernels and brewer's yeast are naturally rich in B_6, but this vitamin is destroyed at temperatures over 245°F. We must get this vitamin from some other source, since we don't eat these foods raw. On the other hand, who can stop eating raw pecans after only one or two? Dr. Ellis's prescription of 12 pecans a day would be an easy, safe and pleasant one to follow.

The Peanut Prescription

Junior is showing good judgment when he insists on peanut butter sandwiches rather than jelly or jam. As a matter of fact, if he must eat sandwiches, peanut butter is better as a filling than almost anything else except meat. Two tablespoons of peanut butter contain more protein than an egg.

In addition, peanuts contain large amounts of B vitamins and vitamin E. They are rich in minerals. Peanut flour is an excellent supplement for wheat flour. It contains four times as much protein as wheat flour, eight times as much fat and nine times as many minerals. In recipes using wheat flour you may substitute peanut flour for 15 to 20 percent of the wheat flour without making any other special changes.

Peanut flour, peanut butter and peanut oil are nearly as nutritious as the raw peanuts themselves. Raw peanuts are far better for you than roasted ones, but you may not like the taste of the raw ones.

Raw peanuts are especially rich in oil which contains the essential unsaturated fatty acids—substances which seem to discourage harmful deposits of cholesterol in blood vessels. Cholesterol deposits are frequently related to hardening of the arteries, strokes, heart attacks and other serious disorders of the circulatory system.

Therefore eat peanuts raw, if you can. If not, roast them lightly. They are good food from many angles. Along with sunflower seeds, they make about the best possible snack and dessert you could imagine.

Many people don't know you can get peanuts that haven't been shelled, deep-fried and salted. Actually, raw peanuts are easy to get in most natural food stores. Try them. It's a treat to get your peanuts in the shell, untouched by any processing.

What about peanut butter? Ideally, peanut butter should be ground raw or roasted peanuts with nothing added. You can buy such peanut butter at natural food stores, or make it yourself. If you make your own just once, the flavor will convince you that you know more about making peanut butter than the most successful manufacturers.

When peanut butter is made commercially, roasted peanuts are ground and salted first. Emulsifiers, flavoring agents and preservatives are introduced. Then hydrogenated oils are added, because natural peanut oils have a tendency to separate from the pulp and rise to the top of the jar. Hydrogenated oils have been treated chemically so that they become solid at room temperature. The solid, hydrogenated oils keep the peanut butter from separating. However there is some scientific evidence that this kind of processed fat is a hazard to heart and blood vessels.

Peanuts and Hemophilia

Our most popular nut is also being investigated by scientists, such as zoology professor H. Bruce Boudreaux, as a potential treatment for hemophilia, an impaired capacity for blood coagulation. Like other victims of this condition, Dr. Boudreaux lives with the ever-present danger that a slight bruise or cut might cause him to bleed to death.

Dr. Boudreaux had been working with several other scientists at Louisiana State University, searching for clues on the mechanics of hemophilia. Various foods—blood pudding, liver, milk and eggs—that might overcome the problem were given to hemophiliacs in large quantities daily. None reduced the severity of the disease significantly.

One day Bruce Boudreaux noticed that a sore knee which had shown signs of causing a severe bleeding problem healed, literally overnight! Clinical symptoms of hemophilia frequently disappear without any apparent outside influence. In such cases the patient may have eaten something that closed, for a short time, the chemical gap in his body's clotting mechanism. Dr. Boudreaux remembered eating a handful of roasted peanuts the evening before.

Dr. Boudreaux began to test the therapeutic value of peanuts. He used them in every available form: roasted and raw peanuts, peanut butter, peanut flour, and even a concentrate prepared from peanut flour. He ate peanuts every time he had a hemophilic attack: in each instance the symptoms went away within one or two days.

The mechanics of how peanuts curtail the bleeding of some hemophiliacs during an attack has yet to be fully determined. Papers which appeared after Dr. Boudreaux's original in (*Nature,* 13 February, 1960) have corroborated his findings on the value of peanuts as a therapeutic measure (*Archives of Biochemistry and Biophysics,* August, 1960; *Annales Paediatrici,* July, 1961). Each of them has discounted the effect of peanuts on the actual clotting time of the blood. Rather, the peanuts' value seems to lie in strengthening capillaries against breakdown, making quick repair possible.

Healthy peanuts in the shell are firm, not shrivelled.

Chapter 8

How To Make Use of Other Nuts and Seeds

J. I. Rodale

Acorn

The following appears in *Seeds—Their Place in Life and Legend* by Vernon Quinn (Stokes & Company): "That same year, 1608, a colonist in Virginia was writing home to London of the strange uses the 'Salvages' made of seeds they gathered in their fall woods and fields. 'The Acornes, being boyled, at last affordes a sweet oyle, that they keepe in Gourdes to annoynt their heades and joynts.'

"Acorns, in those days, were a common food throughout all of America, wherever an oak-tree grew. But the eating of acorns was by no means limited to the American Indians. Today in the mountains of Albania, and in other parts of the world, the poorer inhabitants live very largely on acorns. In Chaucer's day even the upper classes in England relished them. 'Thei weren wont lyghtly to slaken hir hunger at euene with acorns of okes'."

Acorns as food for modern man is discussed in a bulletin published by the Missouri Botanical Garden in 1924. Say the authors: "With modern kitchen equipment, acorn meal can easily be prepared at home. After husking the acorns grind them in a hand-grist mill or food-chopper. The meal is then mixed with hot water and poured into a jelly bag. The bitter tannin, being soluble, will be taken out by the water, but sometimes a second or even a third washing may be necessary. After washing, the wet meal is spread out to dry and is then parched in an oven. If it has caked badly, it should be run through the mill again before using.

"In cooking, acorn meal may be used in the same way as cornmeal. Its greatest fault is its color, muffins made from it being a dark chocolate brown; the taste suggests a mixture of cornmeal and peanut butter, and some people relish it at once, but others, it must be confessed, have to be educated to it. Muffins, $\frac{2}{3}$ acorn and $\frac{1}{3}$ oatmeal, are reported to be good. Because of the high oil and starch content of the acorn, it is very nutritious and is reported to be easily digested. Only acorns from white oaks should be gathered, as those from the black oaks are too bitter."

J. Russell Smith in his excellent book on nut-bearing trees, *Tree Crops* (published by Devin-Adair, New York), tells us that far more human beings have eaten acorns than have eaten wheat, down through the centuries. The acorn was certainly a staple food long before man ever became interested in planting and reaping. One reason for the highly nutritious quality of the acorn as food is its high fat content. As Dr. Smith points out, it is not just bread that you make from the acorns, but bread and butter.

In Europe, chiefly in Spain, Portugal and Italy, acorns are as common in the diet as chestnuts are here. Some varieties can be roasted over the fire and eaten like the roast chestnut. In Spain and Portugal oak trees are cultivated for their acorn crops which sell for high prices in the markets.

Ground acorns are used as coffee substitutes in some parts of the world. Their tannin content is supposed to make them powerful against chronic diarrhea. Of course, to make them tasty the tannin must be removed.

Aniseeds

Aniseeds can be used to flavor applesauce, stews, teas. The Romans ate aniseed cakes to aid digestion. In Europe, especially in Germany, there are cakes with aniseed flavoring. Then there is anisette, a liqueur that is supposed to "warm" the stomach. Anise is also used in soups.

Barley

Barley, a cereal popular in some parts of the world for bread-making, is used in this country chiefly for making beer. Fermenting barley results in malt, a basic ingredient in beer.

Barley is perhaps the oldest cereal food. It was cultivated in China 20 centuries before Christ and was also known in ancient Egypt, Greece, Rome, and among the lake dwellers in ancient Switzerland.

Barley used to have a medicinal purpose—in making hot poultices to apply to infections.

Berries

Strawberries are full of seed. They used to be prescribed for diabetics and heart patients because they are low in sugar. The small seeds exert a mild stimulating action in the bowels. Other berries with seeds are currants, gooseberries, blackberries and raspberries.

Buckwheat

Buckwheat is a cereal almost totally ignored in America. New York and Pennsylvania are the only two states which produce any significant amount of it. The buckwheat flour has a distinctive taste which people either like intensely or dislike just as intensely. Most of the buckwheat grown is used for flour to make hotcakes or pancakes. Unhappily it is thoroughly refined and plenty of other flours such as wheat are added to the buckwheat flour that is sold in stores.

However, for those who like the flavor, there is probably nothing that can compare to a breakfast of buckwheat cakes, made from real, whole buckwheat flour, freshly ground. Raise the batter with yeast to add B vitamins and flavor. Don't think of betraying a wonderful flour like this with baking powder! If you have a sweet tooth, pour some genuine maple syrup over the cakes. This is an almost pure carbohydrate breakfast and we don't recommend it for frequent use. But for once in a while, it's a taste treat!

Many farmers plant buckwheat for its honey. Buckwheat honey has a completely distinctive flavor. After you have acquired a taste for it, any other kind of honey may seem insipid. Buckwheat honey is dark in color and is richer in vitamins and minerals than the light-colored honeys.

Caraway Seed

Caraway was well known to Egyptian priest-physicians before the book of Exodus was written. Culpeper says of it, "Caraway comfits once only dipt in sumgar syrup and a spoonful of them eaten in the morning fasting as many after a meal, is a most admirable remedy for those that are troubled by wind."

Once the seeds of Caraway were prescribed for bringing bloom to the cheeks of pale-faced maidens. You may care to follow the aged custom of Trinity College, Cambridge, where a saucer of these savory seeds invariably accompanies roasted apples. In Shakespeare's *Henry IV,* Squire Shallot invites Falstaff to a "pippin and a dish of caraways." To this day Scots dip the buttered side of bread into a saucerful of caraway at teatime.

Caraway seeds can be used in baked apples, applesauce, soups, goulashes and served to eat as is after meals. Try them with baked potatoes and in salad dressings.

Cardamom

The seeds of the oriental herb, cardamom, have a pleasant, aromatic odor and an agreeable spicy taste. They are used in curries and as spices in cakes, liquors and so forth. In the East they are chewed, like betel nuts.

Coconut

All of the coconut inside the tough outer shell is a seed—the largest we have. Many of the most precious of the coconut's food elements are concentrated in the brown skin that clings so tightly to the white meat, so you should eat this skin when you eat coconuts.

Long ago, coconut meat was said to be very effective for ridding the body of intestinal worms. In tropical countries where it grows, it forms the staple item of diet and contributes generously to the nutrition of folks wherever it is widely eaten.

Coriander Seeds

Coriander seeds are crushed and used in cakes, bread, sausage, cheeses, baked apples, and with game or poultry. They are used in the food industry in making gin and curry powder.

Corn

Corn is America's favorite and most famous grain. The history of corn goes back farther than we have any records. Apparently it was known to the very earliest inhabitants of the western hemisphere. Don't forget how delicious it is raw—right from the stalk.

Cucumber Seeds

Cucumber seeds, we are told, had medicinal worth: "To such as are payned with the cough, if so many seedes be taken vp and vsed at a tyme, as may handsomely bee taken vp with three of the fingers, and these after the bruising with Commyne drunke in Wine, doeth in short tyme amend the same."

Cumin Seed

The fruits (or so-called seeds) of the *cuminum cyminum* are hot to the taste. They contain lots of tannin and are one of the ingredients in curry powder. In olden times they were eaten with bread, wine or water as a remedy for squeamishness! During the Middle Ages this was one of the commonest of the European spices. A stimulant and carminative (powerful against flatulence and colic) it is used today mostly by veterinarians.

Dill Seed

Dill is a delightfully tasty seed that adds so much to pickles, salads, soups, fish, meat, egg and vegetable dishes. Oil from dill has been used in the manufacture of gin. In the East it is ground and eaten as a condiment. Dill vinegar, made by soaking seeds in vinegar for a few days, is relished by many.

Dill is well-known to our ancestors who used to chew the seeds in church. Dill seeds made into a tea are mentioned in a medical botany of the nineteenth century as a cure for obesity. Hiccups could also be cured, it was said, by boiling the dill seeds in wine, then tying them in a cloth and smelling them.

Fennel Seed

Fennel is sometimes made into fennel-water, supposedly a cure for upset stomachs. The seed is supposed to aid in the digestion of beans and cabbage. The volatile oil that comes from fennel is probably the same as that from aniseed.

I ran across a note in an old herb book that fennel tea (made from the seeds) will relieve colic in children. It is good for an eyewash. Fennel also adds to the flavor of puddings, soups, cakes, sauerkraut and spiced beets.

Fig Seeds

Fig seeds, those tiny, crunchy specks in figs, are said to cure constipation. Chew fig seeds carefully to get all the possible benefit from them.

Flaxseed

The flax plant was apparently found growing wild in this country by the early American colonists. Flaxseed oil (or linseed oil as it is generally called) is used widely in paints and varnishes, printer's ink and artist's colors. The oil is used in Eastern Europe as a cooking oil.

Folklore has it that flaxseeds were the source of special magic, which changed as the moon changed. When they were gathered by the light of the full moon, they were used in brewing love potions. On the other hand, if you gathered them when the moon was dark they could do harm to an enemy.

So far as diet is concerned, flaxseeds are a good source of the unsaturated fatty acids so essential to health. They are also reputed to have a laxative effect. Some authorities believe them to be highly nutritious. The Indians of the Andes use them extensively—ground with barley.

In ancient Greece and Rome flaxseeds were a great delicacy, munched between courses of a banquet much as we eat toasted nuts. The herb books tell us that tea made from flaxseed is good for respiratory disorders.

Lentils

The word lens which we use for a ground glass contrivance, was taken from the humble lentil, the sides of which are shaped about the same as a lens. The lentil is perhaps the oldest vegetable cultivated. Well known to all the ancient peoples, it figures in early mythology and superstition.

One historical note concerns the early Christians who were worshiping in the catacombs during the time they were being persecuted by the Romans. They wished to have flowers growing before the altar, but no flowers would grow without light. They discovered that lentils and wheat would sprout and grow in the dark. So these two seeds were annually planted in earthen pots on Ash Wednesday. By Maundy Thursday the plants were high enough to be carried to the altar. Italians still observe this ancient rite.

The old herbalists were of two minds concerning the medicinal value of the lentil. Some claimed it was beneficial as medicine, others condemned it as hurtful. However, we know today that lentils rank high among legumes and that they should form an important part of the American diet. They can be used to advantage in any recipe that calls for dried beans. Lentils mix well with tomatoes, onions, cabbage, vinegar, mustard and mushrooms.

Lettuce Seed

Lettuce seed was a supposed curative for a number of ills, but only if it was used without the patient being aware of it! "The lettuce seeds crushed and mixed with the white of an Egge applyed in plaister forme on the temples or forehead warme at the going to rest dooth marvelously procure sleepe." Lettuce leaves can be used, it seems, in case there are no seeds handy. But the leaves must be pulled up by the root with the left hand, before the sun rises and laid under the invalid's pillow so that the bigger end of the stalk and leaf lie toward the feet!

Mustard Seed

Mustard seed is commonly used today in pickle recipes. The "hotness" of mustard seeds was recognized in the old herbals, for they were used for gargling a sore throat. They "amendeth the blistering of the mouth and asswageth the swelling of the throate. The person which every morning fasting shall swallow down two mustard seedes at a time shall be free that day from the falling sickness [epilepsy]. The pouder of the seedes drawne vp by the nosthrills not onely procureth the creature to sneese, but marvelously purgeth and amendeth the the braine."

Another herbal counsels using mustard seed against dimness of sight and spots and webs in the eyes. A mixture of mustard and vinegar would also quickly cure the bite of a venomous beast.

Or, for those with palsy: "The mustard seedes retained under the tongue prevaile against the palsey of the tongue. The seedes do like profit against all kindes of palseys hapning in any parte of the body if a linnen bag filled with the seedes and boyled in wine be applyed on the grieved place." Even today mustard is highly esteemed for making poultices.

Millet

Millet is a cereal, botanically speaking, although when we speak of it we generally mean any of a number of related cereals. Its origin was probably Egypt. It is used in the form of groats and makes excellent bread, especially when used in a mixture with wheat.

Millet is easily grown, even in very dry or cold climates. It is not used much for human food in our country, but is used extensively in the East.

Nasturtium Seeds

Nasturtium is sometimes called Indian cress. Many people use both the seeds and leaves of nasturtium in salads or pickle the seeds, as one would a small cucumber.

Nutmeg

Nutmeg, used widely today as a flavoring ingredient, had some therapeutic value, according to the old herbals. It was good against freckles and it quickened the sight.

Mace is a part of the nutmeg seed. These two spices have been known in Europe only since the twelfth century, making them fairly recent members of the spice family. They were used to fumigate the streets of Rome during the coronation of an emperor. The Dutch, coming into possession of the island of Banda, enjoyed a monopoly on the nutmeg trade by destroying all trees that happened to grow on any other island. Birds, however, swallowed the seeds of the Dutch trees, excreted them elsewhere and thus spread the culture of nutmeg trees to other islands.

Parsley Seed

Parsley, a plant rich and running over with vitamins A and C, was treasured in the old herbals for its power to "fasten loose teeth, brighten dim eyes and relieve a stitch on the side." We do not know the vitamin content of parsley seed. But the plant itself in large enough quantity in the diet could well provide enough of vitamins A and C to cure a case of scurvy (loose teeth) and night blindness (dim eyes).

Pepper

Pepper is the berrylike seed of the pepper plant which grows in hot, humid climates. The method of curing the pepper determines whether you get white or black pepper. For centuries pepper was in such demand as an herb that it commanded a high price and was often specified as a tribute or fine.

When the barbarian Alaric, King of the Goths, threatened Rome in 409, he demanded a price of 3,000 pounds of pepper, among other tributes.

During the Middle Ages pepper became immensely precious in Europe. Medical men at that time believed that there were four "humors," blood, yellow bile, phlegm and black bile which operated to produce health or sickness in the body. Blood was hot and moist and phlegm was cold and moist. If any one of the humors was out of order, you could repair it by providing a medicine that would restore its original qualities. Hence pepper, being hot, could cure diseases in which the blood was thought to have become cold. It was used, too, for curing indigestion, mistiness of the eyes and other complaints.

How many spices you could afford in your food became a measure of snobbishness in Medieval Europe. We suppose that a large part of the reason for the craze for spices was that there was no refrigeration and little was known about preserving foods in other ways. Spices could be used as preservatives and also to conceal the taste of rancid or spoiled food. Then, too, the perfumes of spices became valuable in an age when baths and personal hygiene were almost unknown.

At any rate, we are told that to this day poor children in some European countries taunt a richly dressed youngster as a "pepper-licker"—a phrase which undoubtedly goes back to the economics of the Middle Ages, when only the rich could afford to have pepper every day.

Peony Seeds

Peony seeds were used as medicinal herbs in Greek and Roman times, and later in Anglo-Saxon kitchen gardens. The flowers were used for flavoring and the seeds were carried as a charm against evil spirits.

According to an old herbal: "It is found by sure and evident experience that the fresh roots tied about the necke of children is an effectuall remedie against the falling sickness (epilepsy)." The seeds "to the number of fifteene taken in wine or mead is a speciall remedie for those that are troubled in the night with the disease called night Mare, which is as though a heavy burthen were laid vpon them and they opprest wherewith, as if they were overcome by their enemies or ouerprest with some great weight or burthen. And they are also good against melancholicke dreames."

Gardeners who specialize in plant personalities will tell you that peonies are extremely sensitive. They grow well only for those who appreciate them, say these experts. They do not like to be transplanted; one of our gardener friends tells us they will grow well only if you talk to them as you would to a child. This gardening lore seems to be tied in with their reputation against psychological ills.

Pine Cones

Dr. Smith in his book, *Tree Crops,* quotes a Dr. Robert T. Morris as saying that nuts in pine cones are near the head of the list of nut foods for

The seeds of the showy peony were once used as a medicinal herb.

human use. Of the 30 species of nut-bearing pines between Quebec and Florida, at least one species produces nuts the size of the average English walnut, while others may be as small as a grain of buckwheat.

Many of the pine trees produce nuts that are edible either raw or cooked. Some of them are rich enough in starch to provide a staple food for natives of South America, South Africa and Australia. Some of the nuts are oily and may be pressed to yield a thick milky substance which can be kept for a long time and used by the natives as a substitute for meat.

We are told that pine cones were used freely by the old herb doctors, for almost any disorder. Fir cones were "wholsom and much nourishing whilst they are fresh, and although they be somewhat hard of digestion yet they do not offend; especially if they be steeped three or fower houres in warme water before the taking, to soake out their sharpnesse and oylinesse."

Poppy Seed

Poppy seed is one of the better-known seeds in this country, since it is in wide use on breads and cookies. The seeds are so small that as many as 30,000 of them can be obtained in a single pod. Opium is not made from the seeds, but from the unopened pods of the poppy. The tradition of sleepiness and death, however, is still associated with the poppy.

The poppy's name came from a custom of giving children the seeds mixed with their "pap," for "the Poppie seedes (after bringing to pouder) mixed with new milke as broth and given to children to drinke warme procureth theme to sleepe." For adults, too, the poppy means sound sleep—"The Garden Poppie boyled vnto the thickness of honey profiteth vnto many griefs. The Seedes confected with sugar and eaten doe marvelously prevaile in procuring the weake patient to sleepe soundly."

Psyllium Seeds

Psyllium seeds, from the plant fleawort, are sold by the drug houses as a laxative. Their action is chiefly mechanical; the seeds swell to create bulk in the intestine (which occurs quite naturally in the digestive tract of anyone who eats foods in their natural state, rather than refined). The seeds lubricate, too, to a certain extent.

Rye

Rye seeds have been found in tombs in association with weapons of the Bronze Age, so we can assume that this is a very old cereal indeed. Bread made from rye flour seems less likely to cause allergies than that made from wheat.

Senna Seeds

Senna seeds were used in olden times for medicine. Infused in whey and then boiled they were a "physicke" against melancholy and many kinds of depression and sadness. Used as a laxative in modern times, they are generally combined with some aromatic herb.

Sorghum

Sorghum is a grain grown in much the same manner as corn. It is hardier than corn in that it will grow in regions that are consistently too hot and dry for corn. In Africa and Asia, sorghum is used as food for both human beings and animals. In this country we feed it to livestock. It is said to have about 90 to 95 percent the feeding value of corn. It should be supplemented with feeds that provide vitamin A and D, protein and calcium.

During World War II, when our sources of tapioca were lost to us, some enterprising food chemist discovered that a certain kind of sorghum could be used to replace tapioca. (Tapioca comes from the cassava plant. It is a root product, not a seed.) So a limited amount of the sorghum grown today is used for this purpose.

Squash Seed

The seeds from all kinds of squash and pumpkins have been known for centuries as good food. The seed of the pepitoria squash has been one of the chief sources of protein and fats for Guatemala's Maya Indians for centuries. Combined with corn, beans, fresh vegetables and fruits, the squash seeds round out an excellent diet and undoubtedly are responsible, at least in part, for the good health, fertility and excellent teeth of these people.

A doctor from the Connecticut Agriculture Station made headlines years ago when he succeeded in breeding a squash whose seeds are "naked"—that is not covered with a tough hull. The gourd-like plant which he developed produced seeds which gave about twice as much oil per pound as the soybean and about one-and-one-half times as much as the cotton seed. Their protein value is high, too.

Organically-grown squash is shown half-hidden by lush vines.

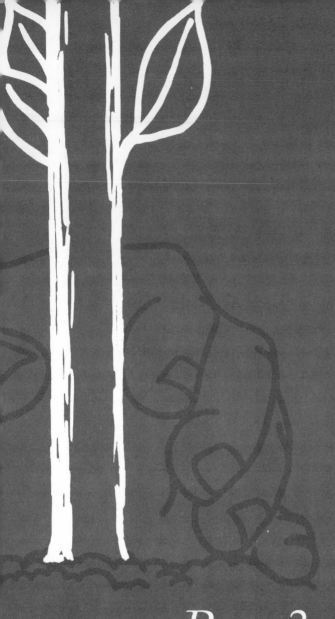

*Part 3
Growing
Nuts and Seeds*

Chapter 9

Growing Nut Trees: Profit without Labor

In ancient times, nut trees had a special name. They were so easy to grow and yielded so bountifully, they were called "profit without labor."

A good many gardeners today are rediscovering the truth of this. Doctors, housewives, businessmen —everybody's getting on the bandwagon and growing nut trees.

The big attraction, of course, is the "double merit" nature of these trees. Besides producing a delectable, highly nutritious crop, they make fine ornamentals. They grow well and provide shade for the front lawn, backyard or anywhere else a handsome addition to the home grounds is needed.

Because of newly developed varieties, you don't have to worry much about the hardiness of the nut trees you choose to plant, even if you live pretty far north. The size of the tree will be the important consideration for most people. You can choose from giants like the black walnut; medium-sized trees such as the heartnut, pecan or English walnut; or comparative pygmies like the chinquapin, filbert or English walnut.

Now that the boom in home-grown nut trees is really under way, the plant breeders can be expected to develop even more varieties. Already they are producing a high-yielding hybrid of black and English walnuts, and one of heartnuts and butternuts. "Hican," a hybrid of hickories and pecans, is now on the market, as is a dwarf Asiatic chestnut which starts to bear nuts when it is less than a foot high.

Here are some useful tips to follow when you decide to grow your own nut trees: buy budded or grafted trees of a named variety; plan on having at least two varieties to insure pollination; and plant late varieties to avoid damage from late spring frosts.

Nut trees generally want a sunny spot and deep, well-drained soil. Use plenty of organic matter in the soil. Avoid southern exposures, except near a hilltop. Plant trees on northern and eastern slopes to help them prevent injury from winter and late spring frost.

Give Them Room To Grow

Give your trees plenty of growing room. A safe rule is to plant them 50 feet apart in all directions. Pecans can be planted 35 feet apart in rows spaced 70 feet apart and chestnuts 30 feet apart. Don't be stingy with growing space. Remember that walnuts, chestnuts and hickory trees frequently tower 50 to 100 feet above the ground, with diameters of 10 to 12 feet. They need plenty of sunlight and air, not only on their tops, but on lower branches as well.

Underground, nut trees compete with each other for the precious soil nutrients: nitrogen, phosphorus and potash. Their roots stretch out in the search for food. Root systems of trees are approximately equal to the size and extent of their branches and leaf areas.

Plant a tree as carefully as you would any prize specimen. Dig a large hole. Holes for walnut trees should be three feet wide and 18 inches deep. Hickories need holes two feet wide and 18 to 24 inches deep. The hole may seem much too large for the tree, but nurserymen have a saying: "Better to set a ten-cent tree in a dollar hole than a dollar tree in a ten-cent hole."

Use good, rich topsoil when filling the hole. This gives the tree a real chance to get started. It will not matter so much later, when the roots extend out into the poorer, surrounding soil. However, lack of fertile soil during the critical starting period can result in the loss of the tree. Settle the roots gently as you replace the soil, and tamp the soil down well. Water the new plant thoroughly, leaving a depression around it to catch rain. Stake the tree.

FOLLOW THESE FOUR STEPS WHEN PLANTING
YOUR TREE

#1

Be sure the planting hole is big enough to take the tree roots without bending them too much. "Better a ten-cent tree in a dollar hole than a dollar tree in a ten-cent hole."

#2

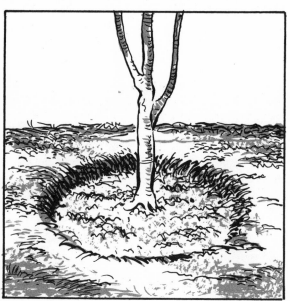

Use good quality topsoil. Fill the hole to within three inches of the top, leaving a depression for rainwater to gather.

Tamp the earth gently but very firmly around the roots, leaving no air pockets. Disturb the roots as little as possible when you are working the soil in around them.

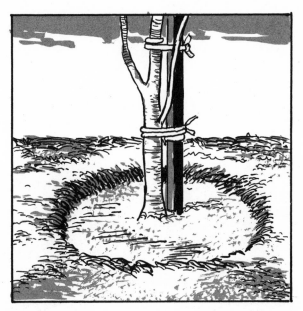

Set a strong stake next to the tree to keep it from falling and to help it grow straight. Take care to make the loops tight around the stake but quite loose around the tree.

Always apply compost and organic fertilizers as a mulch on top of the soil around the tree trunk, preferably in early spring. Try to use a variety of organic waste materials: a frequent cause of nuts failing to make full kernels is a deficiency of one or more trace minerals. Nut trees seem to have a greater need for these elements than do fruit trees.

Wrapping the tree, including the top, during the first winter is another must. This is particularly important with the Persian walnut, which may sunscald. Wrapping also prevents drying out. Regular tree-wrapping paper or burlap bags will do the job. Be sure to remove wrapping only when all danger of a late spring frost is past.

In general, the varieties listed in the accompanying table are those which do best in the North. Many of them do equally well in the South: certain ones have special varieties for warm climates. Check the catalogues for these varieties and for the many new ones being developed.

The Best Nut Trees: Eleven Varieties

Name and Recommended Varieties	Size and Hardiness in Northern Zones	Description, Culture, Remarks
ALMOND *Amygdalus communis* (Nonpareil, Mission, Peerless)	Size of peach tree. Trees have been found bearing in north Ontario.	Will not stand heavy, wet soil. Likes a deep mulch. Space 20 feet apart. Barnyard manure best fertilizer. Begins to bear in 3 to 4 years.
BLACK WALNUT *Juglans nigra* (Thomas, Ohio, Snyder, Myers, Cornell, Stambaugh, Wiard)	To 100 feet and more. To New England and Minnesota.	Stately, splendid lawn tree. Grafted varieties come into bearing in 5 or 6 years. Heaviest bearer of all nut trees. Leaves and hulls make very rich fertilizer. Do not plant near apple trees, azaleas, rhododendrons—has damaging effect on them.
BUTTERNUT *Juglans cinerea* (Sherwood, Buckley Craxezy, Weschcke)	To 70 feet or so. Into Canada.	Lofty, spreading lawn tree. Nuts large, oily, delectable, much used in maple sugar candy. Sometimes begins to bear in 4 or 5 years. Craxezy is thin-shelled variety.
CHINESE CHESTNUT *Castanea mollissima* (Hemming, Hobson, Meiling, Kuling, Abundance Nanking, Reliable, Stoke, Yankee, Zimmerman)	Size of apple tree. To New England and Great Lakes.	Practically blight-free. Decorative lawn tree. Fast grower, needs plenty of moisture. Often bears only 3 years after transplanting. Leave unpruned to make bushy form. Mulch heavily. Very profitable for orchards

Name and Recommended Varieties	Size and Hardiness in Northern Zones	Description, Culture, Remarks
CHINQUAPIN *Castanea pumila, C. ozarkensis*	Shrubby, or tree to 30 feet. To Pennsylvania, lower New England.	The sweet nuts are eaten raw. A handsome lawn specimen. Nuts used by Indians in making bread and drink similar to hot chocolate. Not to be confused with chinquapin oak, which bears edible acorns.
ENGLISH (PERSIAN) WALNUT *Juglans regia* (Metcalfe, McKinster, Colby, Weng, Orth, Morris)	To 50 feet or more. Into Canada.	Plant Carpathian strains in North. Beautiful ornamental, fast grower, heavy producer. Plant only on deep rich soil, 60 feet apart. Begins to bear in about 6 years.
FILBERT *Carylus Americana, C. avellania, C. maxima* (Rush, Winkler, Italian, Red, Cosford, Medium Long, Bixby, Buchanan, Barcelona, Du Chilly)	10 to 30 feet, or as bushy shrub. To upper New England.	One of the best nut-bearing plants for home grounds. Needs good but not overly rich soil; do not fertilize first year. Trim to 1 to 3 stems for lawn tree; let suckers grow up for bush or hedge. Begins yielding in 5 or 6 years.
HEARTNUT *Juglans cordiformis* (Walters, Gellathy, Faust, Bates, Fodermaier, Marvel, Wright)	Size of apple tree. To lower Canada.	Fastest grower—often reaches height of 6 feet in 1 year. Large spreading foliage, almost tropical. Richly flavored nuts, 10 or more to cluster; meats crack out easily. Fine ornamental. May bear 3 years after transplanting.

Name and Recommended Varieties	Size and Hardiness in Northern Zones	Description, Culture, Remarks
HICKORY *Carya avata,* C. *laciniosa,* C. *tomentosa* (Stratford, Glover, Bauer, Fairbanks, Wilcox, Weschcke, Bridgewater)	Up to 120 feet. To Ontario.	Majestic shade tree. May be 15 years old before crop produced. Kernels difficult to extract, but big, with wonderful flavor. Will stand even clay soil if rich. Indians made "hickory nut butter."
PECAN *Carya pecan* (Duvall, Sweeney, Busseron, Greenriver, Posey, Niblack, Major)	50 to 120 feet. Some varieties to Ontario.	Plump, juicy nuts. Fine lawn tree. Mature trees yield from 100 to 600 pounds of nuts a year. Duvall and Sweeney are extra-thin-shelled nuts.
PISTACHIO *Pistacia* in variety (Kerman, Damghan, Lassen)	12 to 60 feet. Southern Florida and the West.	Among the most delicious of nuts. Prefers sandy, deep loams; very drought-resistant. Plant one male tree to a dozen females. Resembles spreading apple tree. Starts to produce at 4 or 5 years. Fruits heavily one year, little the next.

You Will Succeed If You—

1. Plant trees 30 to 50 feet apart; give them plenty of room to grow.
2. Plant on well-drained land.
3. Plant an orchard on north, northeast or northwest slopes.
4. Wrap young trees, tops included, with burlap over the winter.
5. Dig planting holes before the trees arrive.
6. Keep the roots moist while planting.
7. Use good, rich topsoil when filling the hole.
8. Water the trees thoroughly (soak the soil) as soon as the trees are planted.
9. Water thereafter once a week only—but do it thoroughly!
10. Use only compost and natural mineral fertilizers.
11. Take a series of soil tests in the orchard to determine food needs.
12. Protect each tree with a strong wire-mesh circular guard 18 inches high and set firmly into the ground.
13. Make a clear, simple map-plan of your orchard plantings, tree-by-tree.

Make Sure That You Don't—

1. Plant on low-lying damp ground or in "frost pockets."
2. Plant on southern slopes.
3. Remove burlap wrappings until danger from late frost injury is past.
4. Expose the tree roots to the sun.
5. Leave air pockets around the tree roots.
6. Mix manures or fertilizers into the planting hole.
7. Order the smallest trees and expect the best results.
8. Set the tree in the hole as deep as the grafting point.
9. Bind the tree too tightly with wire or strings.
10. Fill the planting hole to the top.
11. Prune the leaders (top-centers) of the planted trees.
12. Use chemical fertilizers.

Retire with Nut Trees

Active people don't want to slide lethargically into a rocking chair when retirement time comes. They want a job or pastime that does more than "keep them occupied," and one that brings in some extra money to add to Social Security, pension or insurance benefits. An investment in nut trees during the middle years will increase steadily in value and begin to pay cash dividends when cash is needed— during retirement.

A person can plant an apple or peach orchard when he is 40 or 50 years old, but fruit trees require more attention for pruning, fertilizing, and insect control. Fresh fruit must also be marketed according to a rigorous time schedule.

On the other hand, nut trees require little care during their early years. There is less risk of losing a major investment due to insect damage. There is no need to climb high ladders to do the picking when nut crops start to ripen; bending at the waist and picking the nuts from the ground is all that is required.

Before the days of old age pensions, black walnut trees were often planted on Midwest farms as a retirement investment. If the owner became ill or died, these trees had good cash value as saw logs. One widow was besieged by furniture manufacturers who wanted to buy the black walnut acreage planted by her late husband, even though the trees were not yet cutting size.

More recently, an Ohio lumberman admitted that he was buying cheap land and planting black

walnut trees for future logging. An Illinois walnut
enthusiast grafted Carpathian varieties high on the
trunks of the wild black walnut trees in his hillside
pasture. He harvests Carpathian (hardy English)
walnuts while preserving, at the same time, the tall
black walnut trunks as future saw logs.

Corwin Davis, a farmer living near Bellevue,
Michigan, started his retirement investment over 25
years ago when he planted a couple of pecan trees to
shade his home. Five years later he planted a few
Carpathian seeds.

The Carpathian seedlings did so well that Davis
planted an orchard of walnut trees. He raised seedlings in his own vegetable garden, then transplanted
them to the nut orchard. He grew more seedlings
than he needed and sold them locally. The young
trees did so well on rolling land that the Michigan
farmer grafted named varieties to them—ones that
had done well in his county.

A few summers ago Davis built a black walnut
huller as an additional investment (Carpathian walnuts drop free of the hull). Now he can hull his
own crop easier and his neighbors pay him to have
their black walnuts hulled.

An added bonus from this investment are the
hulls themselves. They make a wonderful fertilizer
and soil conditioner for Davis' garden.

What is the actual earning power of Davis'
orchard? That can't be determined precisely. But
now that his orchard is planted and almost completely grafted it will require a minimum of care.
Still, the nuts have to be harvested, dried and sold

every year. At 20 years old, a good Carpathian variety tree can produce from 50 to 100 pounds of nuts. One of Davis' first seedlings produced 60 pounds of nuts when it was only 19 years old. The first fall he hulled his own black walnuts he earned $60 extra income.

While there's no easy formula for figuring out an exact retirement plan with nut trees, with a little research some fairly good estimates can be made of what income to expect from a given area. Get some experience in nut growing, if you don't have it already. As you learn you will develop skills and interests which can make retirement time more interesting and more successful.

If possible, have more land available than you think you'll need. Remember that nut trees produce best on fertile farm land, not on eroded hillsides. Thirty or 40 acres is not too much for an orchard. If necessary, while the trees are growing to maturity, cash crops can be planted between them.

Contact your state forestry service or state agricultural college for information on the best varieties for your locality.

Why Not Grow Some Peanuts?

America's most popular nut—the peanut—isn't a nut at all. It's a pea, a member of the bean (legumes) family. But its nutritive composition, texture and flavor is so like a nut that we all think of it that way.

Nut-lovers will be glad to know that peanuts can grow nearly anywhere—even as far north as central Pennsylvania. Spanish red and Mexican brown are the two peanut varieties most commonly grown in this country, and they are planted and grown alike. Both do equally well in the North. Even though the Mexican peanut does not produce as well as the Spanish variety, it has a larger size and superior flavor. This is the peanut that is usually sold roasted in the shell at ball games.

Begin by working the soil in your garden thoroughly. If no organic materials have been added previously, turn in compost, aged manure or leaf mold. In the South, plant kernels at least four inches deep; in the North, one-and-one-half to two inches is best. Shallow planting encourages quick growth and prevents damp rot when there is a cold, wet spring. Plant four kernels to a mound, spacing them about a foot apart. Until the plants themselves shade the ground, it is important to keep the soil about them loose and free from weeds. Cultivate carefully so the thin delicate sprouts will not be broken under ground. When the plants reach a height of 12 inches, they should be hilled, the same as potatoes. Hill the soil high around each plant, then mulch between the plants with at least eight inches of straw or grass clippings. The decaying material not only keeps down weeds, but also adds valuable nutrients to the soil. Thus treated, your plants will need no more attention until harvest time.

Peanut plants have attractive yellow blossoms, borne on dainty stems resembling strawberry runners. As the stems grow and elongate, they turn down and bury their ends in the ground.

If you plan on growing peanuts every summer, select seed kernels from your own crop. These will already be adjusted to local soil, climate and growing conditions. Allow the seed to remain in the shells until planting time, to prevent drying out. The peanut plant itself is a rich source of nitrogen and may be dug under to enrich the patch for next season's crop.

Peanuts as they appear when harvested and set to dry.

Chapter 10

Organic Nut Culture: A Complete Listing

Almond

Amygdalus communis, the almond, is a member of the rose family and very closely related to the peach. Although peaches and almonds have many characteristics in common, they have been separately cultivated as far back as records show. Almonds originally came from North Africa and the Orient, and were known to all of the early Mediterranean cultures. The Greeks grew ten different varieties. The almond tree was depicted in early Greek and Egyptian paintings, and figured in Greek mythology.

Almonds are classified roughly as bitter or sweet, though some bitter may be found on sweet almond trees, and an occasional sweet almond is found on a bitter almond tree. The sweet type is grown for food. Bitter almonds are perpetuated chiefly for their rootstocks, on which sweet almond tops may be grafted or budded.

Like most nuts, almonds are a concentrated form of food rich in protein, fat and the B vitamins. One cup of shelled nuts yields 850 calories. In that amount, there are 26 grams of protein, 77 grams of fat, 28 grams of carbohydrate, 332 milligrams calcium, 6.7 milligrams iron, .34 milligram vitamin B_1, 1.31 milligrams vitamin B_2 and 5 milligrams niacin.

Almond trees are just as hardy as peach trees and, for decorative purposes, they may be grown in any climate suitable to peaches. They have the same winter chilling requirements as peaches. But almonds bloom two to four weeks earlier than peaches and the blossoms may be killed, not only by actual frost, but even by chilly weather at any time after buds form. As a result, the warm section of the Pacific coast where peaches grow is the only part of the country where the trees may be depended upon to produce a crop year after year. Even in California, where almonds occupy the third largest acreage of all fruit and nut crops, few growers attempt their culture without making provisions for heating the almond orchards in spring. If you are a home gardener living in a warm area, almond trees should certainly occupy a place in your planting scheme: but don't depend on them to yield except in favorable seasons.

Varieties of almonds grown in California are chiefly Nonpareil, the best and earliest; IXL, Jordanolo, Peerless, Ne Plus Ultra, Drake and Texas, or

Mission. All of these are self-sterile, so two or more varieties must be planted together to insure a set of nuts. In addition, Nonpareil and IXL are intersterile, and will not cross-pollinate each other. These varieties are all soft-shelled, and will produce in few places in the country, outside of the Pacific coast.

Experiments have been made from time to time by growers in other parts of the country to develop hard-shelled almonds which might be induced to yield crops wherever peaches are grown. These attempts have met with some success, but the quality of the nuts and the consistency of crops has not been sufficient to warrant any extensive plantings. However, a few of these varieties, said to yield as far north as Michigan, are Hall, Pioneer or Ridenhower. The Hall variety in particular is convincing more northern gardeners to try their hand at almond-growing. A dwarf variety has also been developed.

Almond trees need much the same type of soil and culture as peaches. The best situation for a tree is in deep, sandy loam containing plenty of humus. They will not grow in clay, and even a heavy loam is likely to prove fatal. Where there is any doubt about whether the soil is light enough, it is better to plant trees budded on peach stock. Those budded on bitter almond will respond only to sand or sandy loam.

Trees should be given a space 20 to 30 feet in diameter when they mature. In California, young trees are set out between December and the first part of March. They should be planted as early in spring as possible in other parts of the country. When they are set out, the soil should be damp but not wet.

When planting almonds, prune back only the injured roots. Dig the holes large enough to contain all roots that are in good condition, and to contain them without crowding or bending the roots. As soon as they are planted, cut the tops back to a height of 24 to 30 inches. If the side branches are strong, select about three, well-spaced, for the main scaffold branches of the tree. Cut off all others, leaving a stub on each branch about one-fourth inch long.

If the framework was started at planting time, branches need only be thinned out the second winter after planting. Leave no more than two laterals for each scaffold branch after the second pruning. If the tree was pruned back to a whip when it was planted, the whole program is delayed by a year. Trees should start to bear in the third or fourth year after being planted.

Almond trees need irrigation as much as any fruit trees, especially in arid areas. Almonds do not have to be watered where rainfall is sufficient to support shade trees. Crops may be increased if manure is spread under the trees occasionally, but the trees do not respond as dramatically to a regular fertilizer program as many fruits do.

The outer hulls of the nuts split open in the fall when almonds are ripe. When most of the hulls in the center of the tree have split, you can shake or knock the rest out of the branches and gather them from the ground. Heavy rubber mallets may be used for jarring the nuts loose without injurying the bark. After harvest, shell and dry almonds to prevent mildew. Spread kernels for drying in a partially shaded place, and leave them there until the meat is crisp. Store the kernels in airtight containers in a cool place.

Beechnut

Nuts of the American beech, *Fagus grandifolia,* and of the European beech, F. *sylvatica,* were both at one time considered great delicacies. However, the trees are seldom planted for nuts today. Both species are beautiful large ornamentals, which may attain a height of 100 feet and live to a great age.

The beech is very hardy and will grow in almost any soil. It should be transplanted to its permanent place when it is very young, because the beech grows with a quickly-developing, long taproot which must be preserved. When grown in nurseries by professional growers the young trees are frequently transplanted to permit pruning the roots and to make possible their transplanting to the garden.

Beech plantings in the northern part of the country have been affected by a dark disease which has killed off some of the fine specimens. The disease is a fungus which is carried by the beech bark louse. It can be controlled by a dormant oil emulsion spray.

Brazil Nut

Bertholletia excelsa. Brazil nuts, sometimes called Amazon nuts, can be grown in the near-jungle conditions of Brazil, Venezuela and Guiana, but in almost no part of the United States except, possibly, the very tip of southern Florida. The trees require great heat, moisture and rich soil. They reach a majestic height, and have two-foot leathery leaves, clusters of showy flowers with no petals but colored sepals and hard, woody, brown fruits four inches in diameter which are packed with 18 to 24 of the triangular nuts.

Brazil nuts are very rich in an oil, which was at one time expressed and used in caulking ships. One cup of broken nut meats contains 905 calories, of which 92 grams are fat, 20 protein and 15 starch. They are quite rich in calcium.

Butternut

See Walnut.

Chestnut

Within the last half century, the American chestnut, *Castanea dentata,* has been practically destroyed on this continent by a blight which swept through our stately chestnut forests in a very few years, leaving dead and dying trees in its wake. The American chestnut, now only known by a few persistent suckers which die almost as fast as they spring from the old roots, was once an important timber and nut tree throughout the eastern part of the country. It was one of the best of the chestnuts, for size and beauty. Perhaps some nurseryman or botanist will find a strain that is blight-resistant and the species may still be perpetuated.

Meanwhile, a number of chestnuts native to Europe and the Orient have been tried in this country, with more or less success. None have the stately forest quality of our American chestnut tree, but some have been found to produce better nuts. The Spanish chestnut, C. *sativa,* is a 90-foot tree producing large nuts which can be grown in the southern part of the country, roughly in the section which the inferior southern native chestnut, the chinquapin (C. *pumila*) grows. But a hardier and more successful import is the Chinese chestnut, C. *mollissima,* which can be grown in any part of the country that is right for growing peaches.

Chinese chestnuts are larger than the American nuts, and are equal to them in flavor and food value. Chestnuts contain about 6 percent protein, 5 percent fat and 42 percent starch. The trees have a more spreading habit than their American relatives, growing no more than 50 to 60 feet tall, and with an equal spread. Flowers are borne in catkins, male and female in the same cluster. Nuts are enclosed in a prickly bur which opens in fall to allow two or three nuts to drop to the ground.

Chinese chestnuts should be planted on a northern or north-eastern slope when possible, to delay blossoming in spring. Like peaches, their blossoms are likely to open before the weather is warm enough for good pollination and early growth.

Deep, fertile, sandy soil containing a large percentage of humus is desirable. When they are young, chestnut trees are shallow-rooted. Even though they will not tolerate moisture constantly standing about their roots, they are also sensitive to drought. If the top layer of the soil dries out, quite possibly the young chestnut trees may be injured or killed. Moisture-retentive soil, then, is a must. Also helpful is a heavy straw mulch over the roots of the young trees. As the trees mature, their roots go deeper and they are less susceptible to injury from drought.

Although the trees contain both male and female flowers, chestnuts need to be planted in two's or three's for crosspollination. Two different

The prickly outer covering of the chestnut must be handled carefully.

varieties must be planted in the same area or no nuts will be produced.

If the conditions are very favorable, Chinese chestnuts begin to bear within three years after they are planted. Fully mature trees in the warmer sections of the country yield as much as 100 to 150 pounds of nuts per tree.

Chinese chestnuts are propagated principally by seeds. Grafting is possible, and even desirable, in cases where exceptionally good trees are available for scions. But little grafted nursery stock is available, the demand being greater than the supply of trees.

Some Chinese chestnut trees may show a tendency to sucker in the garden. A shrubby plant will result if the suckers are not pruned out. The tree may be attractive in this form, but it is harder to care for than if the suckers are removed to leave a single trunk. The trees may need occasional watering during a dry spell, but need little care other than that after they have become established.

Pick up the nuts as they drop in fall, before they have the chance to become moldy or wormy on the ground. Put them in water after gathering. Any rotten or defective ones will float and should be removed. Store perfect nuts in containers which are not quite airtight to preserve the best flavor. Unlike most other nuts, chestnuts are best stored in a slightly damp atmosphere.

Filbert

Filberts are to hazelnuts what Chinese chestnuts are to American chestnuts—the filberts are imported members of the same genus as the hazelnuts, and produce larger and, in some cases, better nuts than the native American species.

American hazels constitute the species *Corylus americana* and C. *cornuta,* sometimes called cobnuts, or beaked hazelnuts. Both yield thick-shelled nuts growing on shrubby trees or bushes not much more than 10 feet high, and hardy through most of the country. Three species imported from Europe and Asia produce better nuts, but they are more tender than the native American hazels. C. *Avellana,* European hazel, makes a shrubby plant up to 15 feet high with good-sized nuts. C. *colurna,* the Turkish hazel, grows in tree-form up to 60 feet, but it is used principally as rootstock for grafting filberts. C. *maxima,* native to western Asia and southeastern Europe, is the filbert, a tree or shrubby plant 10 to 30 feet tall, with large, well-flavored nuts. Commercial orchards, principally in the states of Washington and Oregon, grow the basic varieties of filbert and their hybrids.

True filbert trees, hardy in themselves, can be made to yield nuts in the East or in the northern states in any sections where peaches grow well, but they must not be depended upon to yield a money crop. As a planting in the home garden, they are attractive, useful and, if planted in favorable positions, will yield well in most years. You can grow filbert trees as spreading, dense-topped shade trees, as tree-clusters, like birch, on several trunks in a graceful arrangement, or as hedge shrubs, useful for screening private grounds.

Filberts bloom early in spring, their catkins developing on the first warm spring days. If the bloom is followed by a really cold night or two, the flowers may be killed and no nuts will set. In sections where heavy freezes are rare late in spring, filberts should bear well most years, provided that winter temperatures do not fall below 15 degrees below zero. Dormant flower buds on the filberts can be killed at that temperature, even in midwinter.

The most satisfactory area of the country for filbert culture is the northern Pacific coastal area, where winters are mild, springs are fairly warm and late freezes are rare. The choice varieties of filberts may be grown in this section. The chief plantings there are Barcelona, a variety which makes a large, spreading, productive tree with large nuts that fall easily from their husks as they ripen. Another popular variety is Brixnut, though the trees are somewhat less vigorous than Barcelona. All filberts must be interplanted with a second variety for cross-pollination, being self-sterile. Recommended varieties for cross-pollinating Barcelona are Daviana, Du Chilly, White Aveline, Du Provence, Monticello and Nottingham. White Aveline is also a good pollinator for Brixnut.

In colder sections of the country, American hazels are more reliably productive than filberts, but many of them produce small nuts which are not worth much as food. If you find a seedling in the wild which produces nuts of a good size, dig suckers out and plant them in your garden. A few named hybrids have been developed and are available from dealers. These are mostly offspring of the hazel varieties Rush and Winkler. Both of these produce fair size nuts, but on small bushes. When they are crossed with European filbert varieties, they may yield hybrids which are fairly hardy, yield large nuts, and develop into orchard-size trees about as large as plum trees. Some of these hybrids are Bixby, Buchanan, Reed and Potomac. Two or more of these varieties should be planted together for cross-pollination.

If the climate is at all doubtful for filberts, plant trees in protected spots with northern exposures in order to delay blooming as late as possible in spring. If you can plant the trees on a slope with good air drainage, they may be further protected from frost damage, as well as winter injury.

Filberts need a very deep, fertile, well-drained soil for long, heavy production. Roots of the mature trees go down as deep as 11 or 12 feet. If the soil is too shallow for deep penetration, growth and development of the tree will halt when the roots have reached the limit of their growth. Since the nuts are produced on new wood of the previous season's growth, a halt in tree growth means cessation of nut production. An indication of the suitability of the soil for filberts is the vigor of native hazel growth. If hazels in the area make only small, shrubby growth, the soil is not deep enough for filberts. If the local hazels are vigorous and tall, the soil is fine and filberts should thrive.

Plant trees in early winter in the warm areas or in very early spring in the cold sections. The distance between trees depends upon variety, as well as on the purpose of the planting. In Oregon and Washington orchards, filbert trees are spaced 25 to 30 feet apart each way. If they are to be grown as trees on your home grounds, they should be given about 25 feet; for hedges, the plants may be set as closely as six feet apart. If they are to provide a small thicket which will serve as a screen, set the plants 10 to 12 feet apart and allow them to sucker freely.

Before planting a tree, prune away as much of the original layered wood as possible. Most filberts and hazels are propagated by tip layering. Fewer suckers will need to be cut away if the remnants of the tips or branches are cut off and the plants set so that roots are given a downward, rather than lateral, direction. Sift soil carefully around the roots, and pack it firmly to avoid air pockets.

All filbert trees should be protected for two or three years after planting. Immediately after they are set, wrap roofing paper or thick layers of newspaper around the trunks and tie loosely, as a protection from sunscald. The same precaution is needed in winter, when reflected sun from snow may raise the bark temperature in the daytime enough to cause heavy damage during below freezing night temperatures.

Cut back trees to 24 to 30 inches when they are planted, to balance roots and top. Complete any pruning and shaping, with the exception of suckering, during the first year after planting. Filberts have delicate bark which does not heal quickly over wounds, so the training should be early and severe. Permit three to five scaffold branches to grow. Crotch breakage in filbert trees is rare, so the branches need not be as far apart as branches on fruit trees.

After the first pruning, little should be necessary except the removal of root suckers, if a tree-form is desired. Suckers must be removed from the point of origin on the roots, and the job should be done several times each season during the first three or four years. Pull soil back around the suckers carefully, and cut them back to the root. Rub off any buds showing on adjacent roots at the same time. Suckers should always be removed before the wood begins to harden.

If you want more trees let a few of the suckers grow after the tree has made enough growth to support them. When the sucker is a year old, bend it down in spring and peg it to the ground a few inches from its tip. A cut or break in the bark where it touches the ground often helps to start roots from that point. Throw a few handfuls of soil over the point at which the sucker is pegged, permitting the tip to remain above ground. By the end of the season, a cluster of roots two to four inches in diameter should have formed, and the tip should have made some growth. Early in the second spring, sever the sucker from the layer. The new plant may remain where it is for another year, or you can transplant it immediately to its new position.

Young trees should be well-mulched with straw, "straw-y" manure, alfalfa hay or residues of leguminous crops. If the mulch is grain straw, add some concentrated nitrogenous material, such as cottonseed or bloodmeal.

Pick up filberts and hazelnuts after they have fallen to the ground in fall. If the gathering is done regularly, nutshells will be lighter in color and will be less likely to mold. After they are gathered, immerse the nuts in water and remove floaters. Dry the balance of the crop by spreading it in a dry room, no more than two or 3 nuts deep, and stirring occasionally. When all excess moisture is dried out, store the nuts in rodent-proof containers at a temperature of 55 to 65°F.

Hazelnut

See Filbert.

Heartnut

See Walnut.

Hickory Nut

The hickories are valuable timber and nut trees of the walnut family. Their genus, *Carya,* includes pecans, as well as half a dozen nuts known as hickories, mockernuts, bitternuts, pignuts, and king nuts. All of these are native to the eastern part of the United States, and all cross-pollinate with ease. As a result there is almost no such thing as a pure hickory, *pecan,* might be found in the wild; yet, if nuts from selected by horticulturists for asexual propagation. Some fine specimens of shellbark hickory, C. *laciniosa,* shagbark hickory, C. *ovata,* or pecan, C.

pecan, might be found in the wild; yet, if nuts from any of them were planted, there would be little chance of getting trees like the parents.

Best of the hickories are the shagbarks, shellbarks and pecan (*which see*). The other species may produce fine timber trees, but their nuts are too hard-shelled or have kernels too small or bitter for use as food. Shagbarks are the most hardy, with a native habitat extending up into Canada. Shellbarks are hardy through the Corn Belt, southern New England and southward. The range of the pecans is usually confined to the Appalachians, the southern plains and southward, though hybrids known as hicans can be grown north of that region. Some of the so-called northern pecans are hardy northward, though they seldom yield nuts except in very favorable locations.

Hickory trees commonly attain a height of more than 120 feet, but they are slow-growing. Male and female flowers are borne in the same tree. The nuts are seeds of a four part fleshy drupe which becomes woody in maturity. Best-flavored nuts are produced by the shagbark hickory, but the trees are hard to propagate and transplant, so nursery stock is very limited. All hickories have a strong taproot which goes deep into the soil. When they are transplanted, this taproot must be transferred intact and must be kept straight, or the young tree will die. This is so difficult to do that it is easier to plant hickory nuts and to graft the seedlings in their places in the field. However, the grafting is so difficult that it should be done by an expert.

If you do buy a tree, dig the hole deep enough to accommodate all the roots without bending them. Take extra care to keep the roots moist while the work is being done. Fill the hole with rich topsoil, but do not use manure near the roots. Tie the young tree to a stake so that the wind will not sway it during its first two years. Keep it well-watered for several years after planting, and place a deep mulch over the roots. If possible, use "straw-y" manure in the mulch, but keep it pulled well away from the trunk to prevent rodent damage. Pruning the young tree is confined to cutting back one-third of the top when it is planted. With no further help, it will form a shapely top which starts high above the ground in the mature tree.

Many hickory varieties have been developed, most of them hybrids. Among the hardiest for northern gardens are Wilcox and Davis, both of which yield nuts of excellent quality. Also recommended are Glover, Kentucky, Abscoda, Romig, Kirtland, Vest and Weiper. It is best to avoid hybrids with bitternut in their parentage, because some, like Beaver, yield inferior nuts. Where grafted trees are planted, bearing may start in five years.

Macadamia Nut

Macadamia ternifolia, formerly known as the Queensland nut, is now being marketed from Hawaii as the macadamia nut, a name which is becoming quite familiar in this country. It is native to Australia, where the handsome evergreen trees grow to a height of 40 to 50 feet in deep alluvial soil. In

Florida, where their culture is being tried experimentally, the trees seldom attain much height, perhaps because the soil is not deep enough for them. In Florida's shallow limestone soil they are sometimes uprooted by heavy winds. They retain their balance better in sandy, acid soils.

Macadamia trees are desirable lawn ornamentals in areas where frosts are few and light. Their leaves resemble dark green, spiny holly leaves, and their panicles of white blossoms are sometimes a foot long. Only a few of the hundreds of tiny blossoms in the panicles ever set fruit, but these produce very hard-shelled seeds an inch or more in diameter, enclosed in a husk. With six to seven months of warm weather, the seeds mature, the husk opens and the so-called nuts fall to the ground. These are gathered once or twice a week over a period of a month or more, and must be thoroughly dried before storage. The seed shells are extremely hard and cannot be cracked by ordinary home nutcrackers. A pair of vise-grip pliers is required for the job. The kernels taste like filberts or Brazil nuts and have about the same nutritional value.

Macadamia nuts, with their hard shells, are slow to germinate under ordinary circumstances. They are more easily propagated if the nuts are stratified through the winter, then planted in individual pots and given bottom heat in a greenhouse in spring. Be careful not to disturb the roots when planting seedlings in your garden. Seedling trees show a variance in form as well as in seeds, some of them being tall and slender, some low and spreading.

They may be grafted by side- or veneer-grafts with scions from some of the more desirable Hawaiian varieties. They thrive in deep, rich soil with plenty of moisture.

Pecan

Carya Pecan is, botanically speaking, one of the hickories, a genus of the walnut family. Its native habitat is the lower Mississippi Valley, but pecans are now commercially cultivated through almost all of the states on the southern border of the United States. In gardens and even in the wild, they can be found up the Mississippi Valley as far as Illinois, Iowa and Indiana.

A long, hot growing season is needed to mature good crops of pecans. In the southern states a season of 220 to 270 days, not only frost-free, but quite warm, is considered necessary to a successful orchard. In these states—the cotton states—southern varieties may be grown. In some of the hot, sunny states, like New Mexico, the total may be cut down to 205 to 215 days. Northern pecan varieties require 180 to 200 days' growing season.

Pecan trees are relatively hardy and blossoms open late enough so that they are seldom injured by late spring frosts. Also, the wood becomes dormant in early fall. The greatest danger lies in early freezes, when fall temperatures drop very low. A tree which could normally be expected to stand many degrees of frost when the thermometer drops slowly may be killed outright if the fall freezes are too severe.

The stately pecan tree adds beauty to any area.

Fruit buds of the southern pecan varieties are more tender to winter injury than those of northern varieties. Some of the southern varieties are Stuart, Pabst, Moneymaker, Success, Schley, Burkett and Texas. The following are some of the recommended northern varieties: Major, Niblack, Indiana, Busseron, Green River and Posey.

The hardy varieties have somewhat thicker shells and the nuts are smaller than those of the southern varieties, but the above northern varieties compare favorably with the more tender nuts.

Native pecan groves are found in deep alluvial soils which, though they may occasionally be flooded, drain quickly and thoroughly. Under cultivation pecans may be grown on a variety of soils which meet the following requirements: soil must be deep to allow deep root penetration; it must be capable of holding moisture; it must be well-drained.

Pecan trees, like the hickories and walnut, have long taproots which develop rapidly in the young tree. When they are very young, the taproots are almost as thick and long as the trunk of the tree, with only a few short feeder roots. After the taproot has made a deep penetration, side roots begin to grow, some only six inches to a foot below the surface. By the time the tree is 20 years old, its branches may have spread 40 feet and its roots will have spread even farther. Planting plans should allow the mature tree spread of 70 feet for branches and roots.

Pecan trees bear both male and female flowers, but they bloom at slightly different times. If you want a crop of nuts you must provide for cross-pollination. In some trees the male flowers bloom early and the female late. In other trees the order is just reversed. It is important to be sure that the blooming seasons of your different varieties complement each other. A reliable nursery can supply information about the relative blooming periods of the trees it sells. If the trees are purchased from a local nursery, they should be suited to the climate of the area in which they will be grown.

Young nursery trees should be dug with at least

three feet of the taproot. Larger trees should have at least five feet of root. Lateral roots are usually trimmed to eight to 10 inches. Dig holes deep enough to accommodate the taproot without bending, and plant the tree one or two inches deeper than it grew in the nursery. Fill the hole with well-pulverized topsoil, tamped and watered to eliminate air pockets. Leave a basin two to three inches deep around the trunk for frequent waterings during the first summer.

Trees with about half of their tops removed when they are transplanted make better growth the first season. The amount which should be cut depends upon the amount of root lost in the digging. After they are set, burlap or building paper should be tied loosely around the trunk to prevent sunscald. Also, a mulch of straw, hay or leaves around the base helps to keep the soil moist between irrigations.

Don't prune pecans until the top has made enough growth to shade the trunk. When a thick top has developed, limbs which are less than six feet above the ground may be cut off, one each year.

Pecan trees respond to fertilizing with manure by yielding good crops which increase every year until the trees reach a ripe old age. Trees not fed liberally are likely to produce well for a while and then decline when they have reached the limit of soil resources. After the first year, apply "straw-y" manure to the root area to build the soil. When the trees are young, spread fertilizer in a zone two to six feet from the trunk. As the tree matures, widen the circle gradually until it is about double the radius of the branches.

When pecans mature the nuts separate easily from the shucks, which contain several nuts. In the South, the early-ripening nuts complete this process early while temperatures are still high enough to shrink and dry the shells, permitting them to separate and drop to the ground.

When the season is cool, or if the nuts do not mature as early, they sometimes do not separate from the shucks by themselves and must be knocked from the branches with light poles. Spread a tarpaulin over the ground first, to catch the nuts as they fall. After they are separated from their shucks, store the nuts in their shells or shell them and store the kernels in glass containers. Since unshelled nuts keep better than shelled, it is better to store them whole in a cool cellar until a week or two before they are to be used. After shelling, they keep best under refrigeration.

Pistachio

Pistacia vera, a species of the sumac family, is grown around the Mediterranean and in southern Asiatic countries. The pistachio tree attains a height of about 20 feet in Mexico and the interior California valleys, but grows somewhat larger than that in Europe. It is dioecious, having male and female flowers on separate trees, and grows well only in fairly arid areas. In some places pistachio trees bear good crops only every other year, the alternate crops being blighted with fruits which lack an edible kernel. The fruits, which resemble wrinkled olives, are red and about an inch long.

In California, the trees are fairly easy to grow,

and do best in the sections which do not have the mildest winters. Varieties considered best for their nut-bearing qualities are Bronte and Aleppo, with Kaz as the pollinator. Unless a pollinating tree is planted with the female tree, no fruit can be set. Trees should be spaced 20 to 25 feet apart. If space is limited in your garden, graft a branch from a male tree onto the female tree. Then only one tree will be necessary. They are usually grafted upon roots of Chinese pistachio, a much more vigorous tree.

Queensland Nut

See Macadamia Nut

Walnut

Half a dozen of our best known and most relished nuts, including English or Persian walnuts, black walnuts, butternuts and heartnuts, are all closely related members of the *Juglandaceae* family, and of the genus *Juglans*. The black walnut, J. *nigra*, is most common in this country, especially in the northeast. It is a handsome, hardy and stately tree, native to all the states east of the Rockies. Black walnut trees produce a reliable harvest of strongly flavored, oily nuts year after year in all sections of the country, except the far south, where blossoming is sometimes too early. The trees are ornamental, and the nuts good, though hard-shelled, and the timber is valuable.

English or Persian walnuts, J. *regia*, are grown mainly on the Pacific coast, except the Carpathian variety, which is more hardy. Most of the English walnut varieties are hardy only where temperatures do not go below 10° below zero, even when the trees are entirely dormant. The Carpathians, however, have been known to withstand temperatures down to 30° below. The *regia* species is characterized by thinner shells which are easier to crack, milder flavor, lower and more spreading trees, and greater tenderness in the fruit buds.

The butternuts, sometimes called white walnuts, are the species J. *cinerea*. These are also native American trees, growing in about the same region as the black walnut. The trees have been greatly reduced in number in recent years because of a fungus infestation, which killed off many of the old trees.

Walnuts on the bough, the promise of a hearty snack in the months ahead.

Butternuts are also hard-shelled and difficult to crack, but their flavor is milder than that of the black walnut.

The Japanese or Siebold walnut, J. *ailantifolia,* is similar to butternut both in flavor and in difficulty of cracking. Some Japanese walnuts are quite hardy, but some consistently suffer frostbite in the colder areas. There is great variation in the size and roughness of the nuts.

The heartnut is a variety of Japanese walnut, J. *ailantifolia cordiformis,* which is more consistently tender, but also yields nuts with smoother shells which are easier to crack. Heartnuts are able to withstand winters which are not too cold for peaches. They may be grown in more protected northern areas and throughout the Atlantic coastal states, as well as in the Pacific northwest.

Black Walnuts

Black walnut trees may be found growing in every country lane through the eastern half of the United States. The best of these trees are on deep, fertile soil, and form a good index to the layers of subsoil beneath the surface. Black walnuts make good shade trees for home grounds. Their branches start high enough so that early and late sun each day can shine on plantings beneath them. The trees grow rapidly in good soil, and an increase of two feet per year is not unusual during the first 20 years.

Black walnuts mature in any area where the growing season is at least 150 days, with an average summer temperature of 62 degrees. Best soil is deep loam, either clay or sand with a clay subsoil, or deep

Hardy and stately, the black walnut tree is native to states east of the Rockies and yields a reliable harvest of richly-flavored nuts.

alluvial soil that is well-drained. They do not succeed on infertile upland soil.

One hundred or more varieties are available for planting, the best of them with comparatively thin shells and kernels that are in large sections. One of the earliest varieties developed is still one of the best—the Thomas walnut. Also recommended for their nuts are Stabler, Ohio and Miller. No variety has yet been developed which is good in every respect, but these are the best of those offered at present.

Seedling black walnut trees if not too big, may be top-worked to one of the named varieties by cleft grafting. Trees as old as 20 years have been worked in this way and, within a few years, were back in full production, yielding good crops of the new varieties.

When the nuts mature and fall from the trees, they are enclosed in a tough green husk which must be removed before they can be cracked. This husk stains your hands deep brown, unless you wear gloves. For best-flavored meat the husks should be removed before they turn black.

After they have been husked, dry the nuts thoroughly. This makes it easier to remove the meat from the shells. After they have been air-dried for about a week, a day in an oven gently heated to below 90°, will complete the process. After that they should be shelled, and stored in a cool place in covered glass containers.

English Walnuts

English or Persian walnuts, have, until recently, been grown only in the warmest sections of the Pacific coast and in the East, south of a line drawn through Maryland and southern Pennsylvania. The best varieties are Placentia, Eureka, Chase or Ehrhardt in southern California; Concord, Payne, Franquette and Blackmer in northern California; Mayette and Franquette in Oregon and in the East. Although all varieties of the tender walnuts require some winter chilling, they will not stand temperatures below 10° below zero.

The Carpathian walnut tree produces thin-shelled, mild-flavored nuts.

Within the last 20 years, new varieties of J. *regia* have been developed, some of which may be grown as far north as Canada, and in most of the northern United States. These are the Crath Carpathians, which thrive in many of the types of soil found through the northeast. The best of the Carpathians thus far developed are Metcalfe, McKinster, Colby, Weng, Orth, Morris and Deming. In quality, size of nuts and ease of shelling, these walnuts compare favorably with the English walnuts grown in California.

Where grafted trees are planted, they bear pistillate flowers by the fifth season and, if older trees are present, nuts may be gathered from the five-year-old trees. But the staminate flowers are not produced until the seventh year, so where the trees are self-pollinating, they will not bear a crop until that time. Carpathian walnuts have been known to produce after being exposed to a temperature of 30° below, and they are quite free of insect enemies and diseases.

Persian walnuts thrive best on rich, well-drained soil which is slightly acid, but they are likely to start into growth too early in spring, and both foliage and blossoms may suffer frost damage. Where hardiness is a problem, trees should not be encouraged to make too much vegetative growth by excessive fertilization.

Butternut

Butternuts are the hardiest of any of the northern nut trees and, if it were not for the fungus disease to which the trees are subject, would be one of the longest-lived. Butternut trees may achieve a height of 90 feet, with well-shaped, rounded heads. They grow moderately well on poor upland soil where black walnut will not grow, but are at their best on slight acid to neutral soil that is fertile and well-drained.

Butternut trees grafted to black walnut rootstocks are said to be more vigorous and disease-resistant than those growing on their own roots. Varieties recommended for superior shelling qualities are Kenworthy, Kinneyglen, Buckley, Helmick, Craxezy, Herrick, Johnson, Sherwood, Thill and Van der Poppen. Not all of these may be available through nurserymen.

Butternuts respond well to feedings of organic fertilizers and to leaf mulches through their early years. Mulch newly set trees heavily as far out as the drip line, but leave a mulch-free circle, two feet in diameter around the trunk to discourage rodents. Prepare soil before planting by incorporating rock phosphate into it as deeply as possible, and apply nitrogenous fertilizer in early spring each year to make the young trees grow better. Every three or four years additional rock phosphate should be worked into the top layer of soil under the tree.

Japanese Walnut

The Japanese walnut makes a good shade tree, even in poor soil, but different specimens show a wide variation in their hardihood. They are not reliably hardy enough to bear yearly crops in areas as far north as New York state. They also show a great difference in their nuts, which are quite similar to butternuts, but are sometimes very rough and tough in shell. They are hardier than Persian walnuts, and hybrids between the two species may yield Persians with superior frost-resistant traits.

Heartnut

The heartnut is a Japanese walnut of a special variety, *cordiformis,* which closely resembles the species in foliage and growth habit, but yields nuts which are smoother and easier to shell. Some of the varieties are not hardy in foliage and growth habit, but yield nuts which are smoother and easier to shell. Some of the varieties are not hardy in the northern sections of the country, but are very satisfactory through the central, more moderate areas. Varieties include Bates, Faust, Fodermaier, Gellatly, Ritchie, Stranger, Wright and Walters. Of these Walters and Bates are hardiest, most productive and are recommended for shelling qualities.

The trees thrive in both clay or sandy soil and make a rapid growth. They do not grow as tall as black walnut or butternut, and are of a more spreading habit. The heart-shaped nuts have smooth shells and a flavor similar to butternut. They are borne in clusters, sometimes as many as 10 on one twig, but the yields are not as heavy as black walnut. Thus far the trees do not have a record for long life. Whether organic culture will prolong their span beyond the present 30-year average, we cannot guarantee, but it is worth a try, because the nuts are superior.

Chapter 11

Gathering and Storing Nuts

Suppose you do raise nut trees and suppose you are not satisfied with the quality of the kernels you gather. Don't blame the trees. You may be handling your crop of nuts improperly from the time you gather them until you store them away in the refrigerator or deep freeze. Properly handled, home-grown nuts will give you a taste-thrill you can't get from nuts you buy in the supermarket.

For example, you've got to be prompt and thorough in gathering and hulling black walnuts and butternuts if you want to preserve their flavor and food value. If you don't act quickly, the bitter fluid secreted by their husks penetrates into the kernels, darkens them and impairs their flavor.

To speed the operation, some growers recommend shaking a full tree. But others prefer allowing the nuts to ripen fully on the tree and fall to the ground. However, once the nuts have fallen, the hulls should be removed immediately, to preserve both color and flavor of the kernels.

Check-Test Establishes Importance of Hulling

Spencer B. Chase of Knoxville, Tennessee, conducted an experiment to prove this point. Nuts were collected from 10 trees. The first batch were hulled

Gathering walnuts on a fine autumn afternoon is a satisfying climax to the nut-growing season.

within a week after maturity. The rest were hulled in equal batches over the next nine consecutive weeks.

The hulled nuts were then stored, cured, and subsequently cracked open for inspection at regular intervals from January through March of the following year with these results:

"Without exception, the first batch of nuts which had been hulled within a week after maturity were light in color, mild in flavor, and could be eaten out of the hand like peanuts."

This was not the case with the nuts hulled later at weekly intervals. These nuts had "darker kernels and suffered considerably in flavor and overall quality." According to Chase, "Almost all the black walnuts which reach the market are in this category, and consumers know only these strongly-flavored nuts."

Removing the Hulls

There are several different ways to get the tough but porous hulls off black walnuts. An old-fashioned corn sheller does a first-rate job. Some dry hullers have a reported capacity of two bushels of black walnuts per minute. Some nut growers spread the nuts on a hard dirt or concrete road and drive over them until all the hulls are mashed, and still others use the family tractor or truck or a jacked-up auto wheel in a wooden trough.

Whatever method you choose to follow, it's best to wear gloves if your skin is sensitive to the acrid fluid secreted in the hulls. It is this staining agent which also penetrates the husks, stains the delicate kernels and impairs their general quality and flavor.

After hulling, the nuts, still in their inner shells, should be sprayed with a hose or placed in a tub and rinsed off thoroughly.

Don't Neglect Drying Operation

Drying-out the hulled, washed nuts is also essential. The nuts should be spread out rather thinly on a dry, clean surface and allowed to dry gradually by exposure to a gentle but steady movement of air. A clean, cool, darkened, well-ventilated attic is ideal. Nuts dried in this way will not be attacked by fungus or mildew. When done properly, such drying-out will result in light-flavored, light-colored nut kernels. For light, creamy kernels, and the best possible flavor, many growers spread the nuts thinly on sheet trays to dry.

Wire trays may also be used, provided the nuts are not piled more than two layers deep. Allow them to dry in a shady place with good air circulation. Some growers use deep wire baskets but they are careful to pour the nuts from one basket into another every four days, to prevent mildew.

The length of dry storage time is also important to flavor. Some growers stipulate that nuts should be kept for at least six weeks after harvesting in order to be properly cured. William S. Weaver of Macungie, Pennsylvania, advises that Chinese chestnuts "should be dried from 10 to 14 days for the best flavor and freedom from mold." Their taste is "much improved over those which are eaten right after they were taken from the tree," he reports.

Other growers prefer using cool, underground cellars for keeping nuts until they are ready to crack and use. They believe that moderately low temperatures keep the oil in the kernel from turning rancid, and that, while an attic may be satisfactory for one-year storage, cellars are preferable for longer periods.

How To Buy Nuts

If you've only recently planted your very own nut tree and are impatiently waiting for that first rewarding crop, or if space just won't permit you to grow your own nuts, these tips on buying nuts will come in handy:

In general, nuts with clean, bright shells are likely to contain good kernels. Shells that are dull, dirty or stained, and those that are cracked or broken are sometimes indicative of defective kernels inside.

Since 1930, there has been a decline in the supply of good uncracked black walnuts, according to J. S. Riegel of Toledo, Ohio because "local people will pay four to five times more for good-quality nuts than the distributors. Butternuts bring even higher prices, and hence are seen rarely on market stands, although this tree is easily grown and quite hardy," he concludes.

Weight is important. The heavier the nut, the meatier the kernel. Chestnuts, for example, can be deceiving in appearance. Heavy weight is the best single indication of a sound fresh kernel.

Good coconuts are relatively easy to choose. First, shake the coconut to determine that it has a large amount of liquid or "milk." This is the most important indication of freshness. Then examine the "eyes," those three small, circular, depressed areas near one end. Eyes should be solid, not cracked or punctured. Finally, look over the entire shell to make sure it is not cracked.

When choosing shelled nuts look for nutmeats that are plump and fairly uniform in color and size. Limp, rubbery, dark or shriveled kernels are probably stale.

Storing Nuts

Generally speaking, nuts lose flavor quickly; they will develop off-flavors, darken or become moldy if not protected from air, heat, light and excessive moisture. Rancidity is the worst problem with nuts. It is caused by the fat in them reacting with oxygen in the air to cause "oxidation."

Nuts in the shell hold their high quality longer than shelled nuts. Whole nuts keep better than nuts in pieces. Unroasted nuts hold up better than roasted ones.

Unshelled nuts keep well in a nut bowl at room temperature only for a short period of time. For prolonged storage, keep them in a cool, dry place.

Shelled nuts will keep fresh for several months when stored in tightly closed containers in the refrigerator. Shelled nuts in unopened cans keep well in a cool, dry place, but will maintain good quality longer in the refrigerator or freezer.

Chestnuts, in particular, are perishable at room temperature, but will keep several months in the refrigerator. Shelled, blanched chestnuts (whole or chopped) may be frozen for longer storage. Pack them in tightly closed freezer containers and freeze

A modern device for hand-cracking nuts, designed to keep the kernels from being crushed.

immediately at 0°F. or lower. Use frozen chestnuts in cooking without defrosting.

Fresh coconuts in the shell retain good quality up to a month in the refrigerator. Containers of ready-to-eat coconut keep best refrigerated.

Peanut butter will keep its quality longer in the refrigerator than at room temperature.

Nut Cracking

There's more to cracking a nut than meets the edges of a nutcracker. Good cracking qualities can be bred into a nut. Growers report that when seedling trees grow up without any help they bear nuts with small kernels and thick shells that are hard to crack. On the other hand, nuts of named varieties, taken from grafted trees, usually have thinner shells and larger nut meats. These are much more easily cracked than nuts from seedling trees.

What's the best way to crack a nut? There's no unanimity of opinion. You can use a hammer with a block of wood or metal, or you can obtain a device specifically designed to do the job.

Experiment a little when starting out with a new variety of nuts. Some varieties are best cracked on the ends, others on the side. Some growers say that you should stand a good-cracking nut upright, so the "stem end" receives the blow. The kernel in a nut thus cracked will usually come out in quarters or halves, instead of being mashed or broken into bits.

Chapter 12

Seed Cultivation and Seed Sprouting

Sesame

If you live in the southern part of the U.S. you can have the fun of harvesting a seed crop from your own backyard: grow sesame!

Sesame is a strong, slim annual growing to 18 inches. It has slender, dark-green leaves and inch-long flowers (resembling foxglove), which lie along the square stem. Sesame may be started early in pots in the North and planted in the garden for decorative purposes, but the seed of this warmth-loving plant won't mature in cooler climates.

Start seed early enough in spring to allow it a growing season of 90 to 120 days of hot weather. Thin-out the plants so they stand six inches apart.

Seedlings require full sun and moderately rich soil. Planted as close as this, the plants grow thick and bushy and shade the soil under them.

Pick seed pods in fall just before the first frost causes them to shatter. Spread them on trays to complete drying, then shake the seeds out of the pods, hull and winnow (free grain from chaff by wind or driven air).

Sunflower Seeds

Mammoth Russian is the variety of sunflower seeds usually grown in the United States. If you want to grow sunflowers for ornamental purposes, however, you will find an enormous variety from which to choose. The Double California is very large and showy. Other, less common varieties, are Black Giant, Silver and Gold, Texas Silver Queen, White Beauty, Sun Gold and Tall Red. One strain has globular heads of enormous size, another produces variegated leaves.

One species has silver leaves, another cucumber-shaped leaves. You can even plant a strain that produces both purple and pink blossoms on the same plant.

Sunflower plants need fertile soil and plenty of space for full development. Make rows as much as four feet apart, and plant seeds two feet apart in the row.

Birds know the real health value of sunflower seeds instinctively. When the birds begin to pick out the seeds from around the rim of the flower head, it's harvest time. The outer seeds mature earlier than those nearer the center of the head. Don't wait for the center seeds to fill out or you may lose the outer ones. Harvest as soon as about two-thirds of the seeds are well filled.

The easiest way to harvest this crop is to cut off the heads with a foot or two of the stalks attached and hang them up in an airy, dry place to cure before attempting to separate the seeds from the husks. If you can't hang the stalks up to dry, spread them on the floor. Air must circulate between the heads, so don't pile them on top of each other—you might end up with rotten plants instead of your hoped-for seed harvest.

Later, when the stalks have become brittle, the fat seeds will separate easily. Hold the head over a pan. Then simply run your thumb lightly over the surface of the head and watch the seeds fall.

If you plant as much as half an acre of sunflowers, you may want to use a screen arrangement made of half-inch mesh placed over a barrel. Grasp the dried head with the seeds facing downward and rub it vigorously over the wire, up and back. The seeds will fall into the barrel. In even larger quantities, a regular farm threshing machine may be used to get the seeds.

An average yield per acre is about 50 bushels of seed, but much higher yields have been obtained under very favorable conditions. A bushel of seed, weighing between 25 to 35 pounds, contains about 60 percent husk and 40 percent kernel.

Grow a Pumpkin Patch

Once a gardener discovers how easy it is to get a good pumpkin crop, he is likely to be hooked on planting a few seeds every year. Why not enjoy the vegetable and then dry your own seed supply for snacking? Planting time is the end of May, beginning of June. Plant slightly earlier in regions south of New England. Press eight to ten seeds into the tops of flattened hills that are spaced six feet apart and mounded with a mixture of garden soil and dried cow manure. After the seedlings sprout and plants are four to five inches tall, thin them out to four or five to a hill. Watch the progress of the vines. If there are any stragglers later in the season, thin plants again to three or four per hill.

Cultivate lightly until late July to keep weeds down. Make sure the plants get plenty of water. If you want to encourage extra-large fruit, remove all but two of the pumpkins from each vine.

As the pumpkins get to football size—in late August—give them a quarter turn so the sides will round out evenly. This is a delicate maneuver and must be done slowly or the stem may snap from the vine.

Pick the crop right after early frosts have killed back the foliage. Fruits that have not turned color completely can be put on your porch or near a window where the daylight will "color them up" in a week or two.

You'll have no problem distributing your pumpkin harvest to family and friends for Halloween decorations and homemade pumpkin pies. And you'll have the added treat of a fresh supply of pumpkin seeds.

Seed Sprouting Unlimited

Long ago someone discovered an added dimension to the flavor and nutrition of seeds—sprouting. A growing green sprout is the source of new taste sensations as well as abundant vitamin power. Delicious alone or as an ingredient of a main dish or a salad, sprouts are worth trying for your family's pleasure and health or as an unusual way to market a seed crop.

Use the best seeds (organically-grown, if possible): alfalfa, lentils, mung beans, garbanzas, wheat, peas, radishes, kale, turnips or any other seeds you wish to sprout. Be sure that your seeds are not treated in any way with harmful sprays or preservatives.

Haunt local restaurants for discarded gallon glass jars that have wide mouths. Cleanse them thoroughly. Next, buy cheesecloth by the five-yard package, and some large, strong rubber bands.

Place one cup of the seed to be sprouted in each gallon jar. Put a square of double thickness of cheesecloth over the opening. Secure it with a rubber band and fill the jar half full of water. Let it stand overnight.

In the morning, drain off this water and rinse seeds with fresh water. After pouring this rinse off, set the jar inverted—but lightly tipped—so that the water surplus may drain, also admitting air to the seeds.

A slightly warm, dark cupboard, or a deep laundry sink which can be darkened to keep out light, is a good place for the sprouting to begin. Twice each day, morning and night, give the seeds a fresh-water rinse and again invert the jar in the cupboard. You will begin to see the tiny seed life in a few days.

Different seeds need different lengths of time to sprout. Allow a week for preparation of alfalfa sprouts. Most others take a shorter time.

The fresher sprouts are, the better for the salad-and-sandwich-eater. The best time to eat sprouts is as soon as the tiny green leaves appear. After they sit in a cup in the refrigerator for several days, they become stale, though not spoiled.

Sprouts are a wonderful, live food. You owe it to your family to have sprouts available throughout the year. Seeds for sprouting and patented growing kits are available in most health food stores.

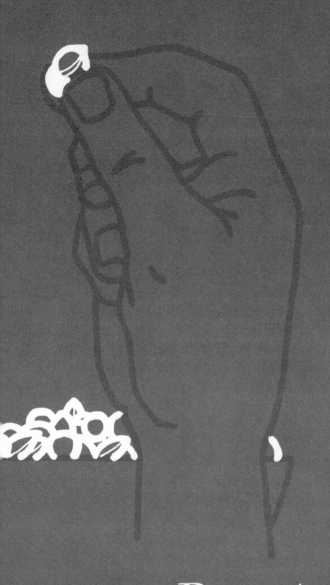

Part 4
Snacking with Nuts and Seeds

Chapter 13

How To Get The Nuts-and-Seeds Habit

Substitute nuts and seeds for candy, cake and soda when you're preparing snacks. Get into the habit of sprinkling ground sesame, sunflower seeds or nuts over salads, vegetable dishes and fruit cups. Nut flours and nut meals make exceptionally nutritious bread or porridge. Almond meal, containing no starch and very little sugar, is frequently used as a flour in bread for diabetics. Nut butters provide another tasty way to take advantage of these tree-borne foods.

Have an attractive bowl of nuts, with a nut-cracker, ready on your living room table. Keep a jar of tasty seeds handy to munch on when the children clamor for sweets and friends drop-in. Serve them just as they are; skip all the roasting, frying and salting processes which do nothing but detract from the nuts' and seeds' nutritional value.

According to nutrition expert, Dr. J. H. Kellogg, "They (nuts) supply for a given weight nearly twice the amount of nutriment of any other food."

Homemade Nut Butters—Fast and Flavorful

At the flip of a switch you can treat your family to nut butter made in your own kitchen. If you have

A bowl of nuts makes an attractive and enjoyable party snack.

an electric seed grinder, put it to use. Make small batches of nut butters without questionable additives and enjoy them freshly made.

Use raw peanuts, walnuts, almonds, cashews, pecans, hickory, filberts or whatever nuts you fancy. Raw seeds, such as sesame, sunflower or pumpkin work equally well. Grind only a few tablespoons at a time, and keep emptying the nut meal into a mixing bowl until you finish grinding. An electric blender will work if you don't have an electric seed grinder, however the meal will be somewhat coarser. If you do use a blender, flip the switch on and off several times. While it's off, use a rubber spatula to keep working the meal down the sides of the container, toward the blades, until the nuts are ground. With either machine, allow time between grindings to cool the motor.

If you plan to make nut butter in greater quantity than for a family meal or snack, use the special "worm-gear" for oily substances. It comes as an attachment with some meat or grain grinders.

Add vegetable oil to the meal to make it spreadable. How much oil? It depends. Some nuts, such as walnuts, are quite oily; others, like cashews, are relatively dry. The ratio is approximately one tablespoonful of oil to each five tablespoonsful of nuts or seeds. Experience will guide you. If you find that you've been overly generous with the oil and have a thin mixture, simply add more meal. Using a flexible spatula, blend the mixture thoroughly.

Be guided by your individual preference in choosing the kind of oil you use. Just be certain to use oil that is fresh and unrefined. After blending the nut meal and oil, your butter is ready to use—made in a jiffy! Keep fresh, untreated nut butters in the refrigerator to avoid rancidity and preserve flavor.

Save, beg or buy small jars with wide mouths. Pack nut butter into them, add homemade labels, wrap attractively, and present them to friends or neighbors. Such gourmet gifts may serve as an introduction to the delicious and nutritious world of natural foods: no fillers, no emulsifiers, no hydrogenated fats, no artificial flavors or colors, no antioxidants—just honest-to-goodness nut butter to tempt the palate!

You may wish to experiment with variations on your basic nut butter. Try adding one of the following: a dash of kelp or salt, brewer's yeast, powdered bone meal, or a pinch of organic dried soup mix. Or you might enjoy adding a bit of honey, carob powder, dried, shredded, unsweetened coconut, or minced, dried fruit.

If you are unaccustomed to the flavor of raw peanuts, you may find homemade peanut butter "beany." Try roasting one-fourth of the peanuts lightly in your oven. When they are cool, grind them together with the raw nuts. You'll discover that the roasted flavor permeates the butter. According to the USDA's *Composition of Foods, Handbook #8,* there is not very much difference in the food value between roasted and raw peanuts.

If you find brown sesame nut butter too bitter, use the hulled seeds. To remove the skins of almonds, which have some prussic acid, blanch by pouring hot water over them. Then, hold the nut firmly between your thumb and index finger, and it will pop out of its brown jacket. Dry the almonds on paper toweling before grinding them.

Broken pieces of nutmeats and cashew halves, are usually cheaper than whole nuts, and economical for making nut butters. Make certain that the pieces are fresh and not rancid.

You will discover that homemade nut butters have a rougher consistency than those commercially prepared. This is no drawback. Most people seem to enjoy the texture and chewiness. Homemade butters have what advertising agencies like to call "spreadability" and are really easy to use.

Are you trying to decrease your intake of saturated fats by substituting more unsaturates? Try using nut butter as a sauce on your steamed vegetables. Want to reduce or eliminate bread and crackers from your diet? Spread nut butters on thinly sliced rounds of raw white turnip, yellow rutabagas, carrots or cucumbers.

Are you interested in new ideas for delicious no-fuss snacks? Fill hollow celery stalks with nut butter for a nutritious appetizer. Remove the pits from dates and stuff the cavities with nut butter. Or chill the butter, then shape about a teaspoon of it into a ball between your palms. (Wet palms frequently in cold water.) Roll nut butter balls in whole sesame seeds or dried and shredded, unsweetened coconut. Arrange them on a platter, spear each with a toothpick and chill before serving.

Chapter 14

Add a Little Health to Your Next Party

Even those of us who watch the kind of foods we eat 52 weeks out of the year, often let down our guard when it comes to giving a party. We think we owe it to our friends to serve what they are used to.

If you have been changing your snacking habits to eliminate the empty-calorie junk foods from your diet, what can your serve to your guests that will look irresistible and taste so good that they'll never realize that there were no pretzels, potato chips, corn curls or gum drops at your party? Plenty. And these unexpected treats may be the difference between an ordinary party and a memorable evening. Everyone likes new experiences; delicious and unusual foods are always reliable as conversation starters.

Try these:

Tidbits

Honey-coated pumpkin seeds will be a big hit with your guests. They are tastier and much more interesting than candy-coated peanuts. To make them yourself is unnecessarily time consuming. You can buy them at most natural food stores. Also, pick up some carob bars while you're there. Carob has a flavor similar to chocolate, but is more creamy and mild. Other candies, sweetened with honey, are also available.

Perhaps you would like to make some "Nutty" candies, too. Here are four recipes for you to consider:

Sunflower Seed Rolls

2 cups sunflower seeds
1 tbsp. honey
1 tbsp. peanut butter
dash of vanilla
grated coconut, wheat germ or dried fruit*

Blend sunflower seeds to a fine meal. Start with the blender lid on and then remove lid and push seeds down with a spatula. Always do this carefully, keeping far away from the cutting blade. Add honey to one cup of the ground seeds; peanut butter and vanilla to the other cup. Knead into dough, form into balls or desired shapes and roll in one of your favorite coating mixtures.*

* Grated coconut; chopped, dried fruit; wheat germ, etc.

Sesame Seed Specials

2 cups sesame seeds
½ cup soy, corn or safflower oil
2 tbsp. honey
dash of vanilla
1 tbsp. peanut butter
1 tbsp. carob

Blend seeds with oil. Add honey and vanilla to running blender. Blend until smooth. Divide into three bowls. Add peanut butter to one, carob to the second. Leave one plain. Shape into balls. Do not coat these. They resemble fudge.

Sesame Taffy

1 cup sesame seeds
½ cup soy, corn or safflower oil
honey to taste
dash of vanilla
dash of natural almond flavoring

Blend seeds with oil. Add remaining ingredients. Let blender run a long time until mixture gets hot and looks glossy. Turn out into bowl. With rubber scraper knead up on side of bowl, squeezing out the oil. Finish kneading with your hands, squeezing out the oil. Roll this dough into a log and slice. (Save sesame seed oil for making Pumpkin Seed Candy.)

Pumpkin Seed Candy

In blender:
2 cups pumpkin seeds
½ cup of oil from Sesame Taffy
2 tbsp. honey
dash of pure vanilla

Drop by teaspoons into coating mixtures. Chill.
Freeze separately on a cookie sheet. Then place
in freezer containers to store in the freezer.

The nicest way to say "welcome" to your guests
is with an interesting dip that's tangy, nutritious and
delicious, but not filling:

Yogurt-Walnut Dip

1 clove garlic
2 or 3 walnuts
1 tsp. olive or soy oil
salt
paprika
dash of vinegar or lemon juice
1 cup thick yogurt
diced cucumber

Blend ingredients the afternoon of your party.
The flavors meld together well in the refrigerator.

Sesame Seed Yogurt

This yogurt is made much the same as cow's
milk yogurt. Add yogurt culture to sesame seed milk
and let it stand overnight in a warm place for about
12 hours.

The following two recipes are particularly high in the nitrilosides:

Blender Apricot Jam

¼ cup roasted apricot kernels
1 tbsp. or more honey
1 cup pineapple juice
1 tbsp. lecithin granules (optional)
dried apricots, enough to thicken jam

Grind kernels in a small nut mill or in the blender. Place all other ingredients in the bowl and slowly add enough dried apricots to make a thick jam. Mint leaves may be used to vary this recipe or 1 tbsp. grated orange rind. Store jam in a covered jar and keep refrigerated.

Make peach jam in the same way using dried peaches and roasted peach kernels.

Cranberry Relish

1 cup apple or pineapple juice
1 lb. fresh, raw cranberries
2 large apples, washed and stemmed
2 large pears, washed and stemmed
2 tbsp. honey
¼ cup apricot kernels, finely ground or
  chopped

Place juice in blender bowl, then grind the fruits a few at a time in the juice. Strain juice and repeat until all fruit is chopped. Drain and reserve juice for a beverage. Add honey and ground apricot kernels. Mix well and let stand overnight to permit the flavors to blend. Refrigerate until ready to serve.

You can choose from a large variety of spreads and butter at your local natural food store—or you can make your own.

Sesame butter makes a tasty spread, but its flavor will be foreign to most palates. If your guests are not very adventurous about food, better stick with cashew and almond butter and the sugar-free preserves.

Crackers for your spread which are free of all undesirable ingredients are difficult to buy. You may find it simpler to choose one of the following recipes and try your hand at making them. Mixing them will not take long and, if made in quantity they will be less expensive than if you were to buy them.

Corn Meal Crackers

1 cup yellow corn meal
½ tsp. salt
1 tbsp. soy, corn or safflower oil
⅞ cup boiling water
¼ cup sesame seeds

Combine ingredients. Drop by tablespoons on oiled baking sheet. Spread in 3-or-4-inch rounds. Bake at 400°F. until golden. Poppy or other seeds may be substituted for the sesame seeds.

Canapé Crackers

(Good with soup or jam, too)

1½ cups soy flour
1½ cups corn flour
¼ cup soy or corn oil
½ cup water (least bit less than ½)
2 eggs (beaten)

Sift soy and corn flour into mixing bowl. Make a well in center and pour in oil, water and beaten eggs. Stir until it forms a ball of dough. (Should be slightly moist, not dry. If necessary, add a bit of water.) Pinch off pieces and shape into 1-inch balls; set on greased or oiled cookie sheet and flatten. Bake at 325°F. for 10-12 min.

Corn Crisp Crackers

1 cup stone ground corn meal
1 tbsp. soy, corn or safflower oil
½ tsp. kelp
⅞ cup boiling water

Combine all ingredients. Make balls using 1 tablespoon mixture for each. Place on oiled baking sheet, and pat or mash into 3-inch rounds. Bake in hot oven (400°F.) for 30 min. Makes 2 doz.

Oatmeal Crackers

1 cup potato water
½ cup soy, corn or safflower oil
1 tsp. salt
4 cups quick-cooking oatmeal
caraway seeds

(You can use old-fashioned rolled oats instead and whiz them up fairly fine, a cup at a time, in the blender.) Mix the ingredients, except the caraway seeds, into a stiff dough and chill it in the refrigerator. Lightly flour a board and roll the dough very thin. Sprinkle with caraway seeds and roll them in. Now transfer the thin pastry to an oiled cookie sheet. Cut in squares and prick with fork tines. Bake at 350°F. about 20 min.

Corn Chips

2 cups corn meal
3 tbsp. raw peanut flour
½ tsp. salt
1½ cup boiling water
4 tbsp. corn oil

Put corn meal in mixing bowl. Mix in peanut flour and salt. Add boiling water, gradually. Dough should be moist, but not sticky. Add corn oil and mix thoroughly. Cover bowl and allow mixture to cool for about an hour. Form into patties and lay on oiled cookie sheet. Bake in 375°F. oven until edges are brown, about 45 to 50 min. These make ideal snacks and can be used as a bread substitute.

Sesame Seed Cheese

First make a sesame seed clabber by letting the sesame seed milk stand overnight in a warm place to sour. You might add some lemon juice to hasten the souring process. Clabber should be ready in 24-36 hours. Put the clabber in a cloth bag and hang it overnight, the same as when making cottage cheese from sour milk. Collect the whey in another utensil. The whey can be used in baking goods as a leavening agent.

When your cheese is ready, try adding chives, green onion tops, a good vegetable seasoner, or some caraway seeds. Makes a zippy spread.

You may have occasion to prepare a Sunday-morning or holiday-morning brunch for guests. A big bowl of nutty, moist granola, would be appealing to both children and adults. You can make it ahead of time, by the gallon. Then, just set out a big, pretty bowl of granola surrounded by a choice of one or two nut milks, along with the regular kind, and invite your guests to mix and munch.

Granola Cereal Mix

Mix lightly in a bowl:

½ cup sunflower seed meal or any nut meal
1 cup corn flour
3 qt. oatmeal
½ cup unsulphured dates or figs, chopped
½ cup sun dried, seedless, unsulphured
    raisins, chopped
½ cup coconut, unsweetened
½ cup soya flour
1 cup stone-ground corn meal
1 cup nuts, chopped
    (pecans, walnuts or peanuts)
½ cup seeds such as sesame, sunflower or
    pumpkin
¼ cup wheat germ

Then mix:

½ cup date sugar
1⅓ cups water
⅔ cup honey
1⅓ cups sesame seed oil

Combine mixtures. It should be moist, chunky and crumbly. If too moist, add more oatmeal.

Spread thin on cookie sheet. Bake 1 hour at 225°F. or until light brown.

Serve with warm, homemade applesauce to which a dash of cinnamon has been added, or with any chopped or sliced fresh fruit or canned fruit. Serve as a cold cereal with milk. Makes enough to fill a gallon container.

Here are recipes for some different kinds of nut milk:

Sesame Milk

3 cups water
1 cup sesame seeds
1 tbsp. soy flour
carob or honey, to taste

Blend $\frac{1}{2}$ cup of sesame seeds with 1 cup of water. Strain through cheese cloth. Now blend the other $\frac{1}{2}$ cup of seeds with the second cup of water and strain. Add the last cup of water to the whole. Add the soy flour for more body and extra nutrients and either carob or honey to taste.

Peanut Milk

½ cup peanuts, shelled and skinned
2 cups water
blackstrap molasses or honey, if desired

Blend peanuts and water until the nuts are mostly reduced to fine pulp. Add blackstrap molasses or honey if desired, but peanut milk usually needs no sweeteners. You can strain the peanut milk through a wire strainer or cloth. The chunks which remain are fine to eat with a spoon.

You can reduce hard nuts quicker if you put $\frac{1}{4}$ cup of nuts and $\frac{1}{2}$ cup water in the bottom of the blender and reduce the nuts to pulp, then add the remainder of the water and blend again.

If you don't have a blender, take a tablespoon of homemade peanut or nut butter and stir it into a cup of warm water.

Almond Milk

1 cup almonds
2–4 cups water

Blend almonds with small amount of water, then add additional water to desired thickness. A little water will give you almond butter, more will give you almond cream and still more will give you almond milk.

Follow the same procedure for cashew milk.

Sunflower-Date Loaf

1 yeast cake
1 cup lukewarm water
2½ cups whole wheat flour
¾ cup seeded dates, chopped
½ cup date sugar or honey
2 egg yolks, beaten
¾ cup sunflower seeds, coarsely chopped
½ tsp. salt
½ tsp. cloves
1 tsp. cinnamon

Dissolve yeast in water, add 1 cup flour and mix until spongy. Let rise until light and frothy. Add remaining ingredients and blend into spongy mixture. This becomes a fairly firm loaf. Spoon into greased loaf pan or bread tin, let rise until nearly doubled. Bake at 375° F. at least 45 min.

Pineapple Porcupines

1 pineapple
1 cup honey
1 cup wheat germ, sunflower or sesame
   seeds

Remove eyes of peeled pineapple with paring knife and cut pineapple into pieces approximately 2 inches square. Insert toothpick into each square to act as a handle. Now dip the cubes into the honey, then roll them in the wheat germ, sesame seeds or sunflower seeds. You may put them on a tray in the freezer to harden until snack time, or serve all ingredients on your cocktail table as a "do-it-yourself" dip. This one is especially refreshing in warm weather.

Peanut-Raisin Cookies

½ cup wheat germ
½ cup soy flour
2½ cups oatmeal
1 tbsp. baking yeast
½ tsp. salt
¾ cup raw peanuts, chopped
⅓ cup soy, corn or safflower oil

⅔ cup honey, blackstrap molasses
   or sorghum
2 eggs
½ cup apple or pineapple juice
1 tsp. pure vanilla
½ cup raisins

Mix dry ingredients well (wheat germ, soy flour, oatmeal, yeast, salt, peanuts). Set aside.

In a large bowl beat together oil and honey, molasses or sorghum. Add eggs, beat again. Then add juice, vanilla and raisins. Mix well. Add dry ingredients to liquid mixture and mix well. Let batter rest 20 min. before baking. Drop by teaspoons onto oiled cookie sheets. Bake at 375° F. 10-15 min. or until golden brown.

Soy-Walnut Cookies

½ cup honey
½ cup blackstrap molasses or sorghum
4 egg yolks
1 cup raisins
2 cups walnuts, broken
¾ cup soy flour
1 tbsp. cinnamon
4 egg whites, beaten

Cream honey, molasses, yolks; fold in raisins, walnuts, flour and cinnamon. Then fold in beaten egg whites. Spread on oiled cookie sheet. Bake 20 min. at 350° F. Cut into strips when cool.

Carob Brownies

½ cup honey
2 tbsp. blackstrap molasses or sorghum
¼ cup sunflower seed oil
2 eggs, separated
½ cup soybean powder
½ cup sunflower seed meal
½ cup carob powder
½ tsp. allspice (optional)
½ tsp. ginger (optional)
1 tsp. cinnamon (optional)
1 tsp. pure vanilla
    (can be used in place of spices)
½ cup raisins or dates, chopped

Use 3 sizes of mixing bowls. In the largest bowl, mix honey, blackstrap molasses or sorghum, and sunflower seed oil. Beat egg yolks and add to mixture.

Beat the egg whites (stiff, but not dry) in the smallest bowl and set aside.

In the medium-sized bowl, combine soybean powder, sunflower seed meal, carob powder, and vanilla or spices. Add this mixture to large bowl, a little at a time. This will be very stiff. Then add raisins or dates and mix well. Add beaten egg whites to mixture.

Pour into oiled 9-inch square pan. Bake at 350° F. for 25 min. Cool: cut into squares.

Index

Other ORGANIC LIVING PAPERBACKS from RODALE PRESS

☐ **ORGANICALLY GROWN FOODS: WHAT THEY ARE, WHY YOU NEED THEM by the Staff of** *Organic Gardening and Farming*®. Explains how organically grown foods are distinguished from other foods and why they are the most beneficial foodstuffs available. Included are chapters showing how to get better nutrition for the food dollar, how to combine organically grown foods into tasty meals, and how to relate food and farming to solve present-day social ills.
($2.95)

☐ **THE ORGANIC DIRECTORY by the Rodale Press Editorial Staff.** A handbook for organic living, this book not only defines the word "organic" and its applications but also presents practical information to facilitate and enhance the reader's enjoyment of natural living. Included in the detailed appendix are the addresses, listed by state, of organic garden suppliers, stores stocking organic fertilizers, organic gardening club centers, and ecology action group headquarters. ($2.95)

☐ **THE NATURAL BREAKFAST BOOK by the Editors of Rodale Press.** Can you remember a real breakfast—a breakfast before the days of sugar-coated cereals, jam-filled toaster snacks and breakfasts-in-a-packet? Here is a reevaluation of the importance of breakfast and a reintroduction of breakfast as a creative eating adventure. Outlines breakfast menus and provides recipes using completely natural ingredients.
($2.95)

☐ **ORGANIC FERTILIZERS: WHICH ONES AND HOW TO USE THEM by the Editors of** *Organic Gardening and Farming*®. Explains J. I. Rodale's theory for treating soil as a living organism needing nourishment. To support their growth, plants extract organic matter from the soil, and to maintain the natural balance of the soil's composition, it is necessary to return organic matter to the soil in the form of organic fertilizer. This book tells which fertilizers to choose and how and when to apply them. ($2.95)

RODALE PRESS BOOK DIVISION

Dept NS
Emmaus, Pa. 18049

Please send me the Organic Living Paperbacks I have checked above. I enclose $_____ (check or money order) which includes 25¢ a copy to cover handling and mailing costs. (Prices are subject to change without notice.)

Name _____

Address _____

City_____ State_____ Zip Code_____

Please allow at least 3 weeks for delivery

Other ORGANIC LIVING PAPERBACKS from RODALE PRESS

☐ **COMPOSTING: A STUDY OF THE PROCESS AND ITS PRINCIPLES by Clarence Golueke, Ph.D.** A thorough examination of the laws and technology of composting science. Presents an in-depth discussion of the two most commonly used modern composting methods: University of California and Indore (Sir Albert Howard) techniques, and offers suggestions for the home composter. In addition, the book's introduction gives a brief history of the progress of composting skills since 1950. ($2.95)

☐ **GETTING THE BUGS OUT OF ORGANIC GARDENING by the Staff of *Organic Gardening and Farming*®.** This book will help the gardener eliminate pests without disturbing ecological balances. Organic gardeners share their home-tested recipes for safe and sane insect control without chemicals. Contains a guide to signs of common garden pests, a list of insect-deterrent herbs and plants, and specific alternatives to synthetic sprays. ($2.95)

☐ **THE NATURAL WAY TO A HEALTHY SKIN by the Editors of *Prevention*®.** A clear case for sound eating habits and the use of skin products made exclusively from natural sources. Details the dramatic results produced by nutrients, such as vitamin A, in the relief of various skin diseases. Outlines formulas for beauty aids, explains which foods to avoid, and tells which cosmetics may cause baldness and other skin ailments. ($2.95)

☐ **THE NEW FOOD CHAIN: AN ORGANIC LINK BETWEEN FARM AND CITY by Jerome Goldstein of *Organic Gardening and Farming*®.** Reveals the interdependence of farm and city, and illustrates how organic living can cause closer communication between the two. This book represents the collective knowledge of ten experts with diverse specializations: architecture, farming, biology, economics, ecology, writing, and nutrition. Concludes that, organically, the link between city and farm can be strengthened to resolve certain ecological and economic problems. ($3.95)

RODALE PRESS BOOK DIVISION

Dept NS
Emmaus, Pa. 18049

Please send me the Organic Living Paperbacks I have checked above. I enclose $_____ (check or money order) which includes 25¢ a copy to cover handling and mailing costs. (Prices are subject to change without notice.)

Name _____

Address _____

City_____ State_____ Zip Code_____

Please allow at least 3 weeks for delivery